If this book had been around in my ¦
would have helped me understand tl
the work-life balance God wanted for me, and have p—
from becoming yet another casualty of the conflicting pressures
life brings. The aptly named *Get a Life* is extremely readable and
potentially life-changing, full of real-life cameos and helpful supporting scriptures. It is a 'must read' for all those who want to live
the life God wants for them.
Steve Bradley, Chairman of CWR

Many of us spend the majority of our waking hours in the workplace – an arena that presents daily challenges for our Christian
faith. So *Get a Life* will be a welcome help for many Christians.
What I particularly appreciate about the book is the way it roots
our work life in our new identity in Christ. This is what will make
the difference on the factory floor or in the office cubicle – not a
set of rules or clichéd aphorisms.

But rooting behaviour in our identity in Christ can often sound
vague. The great thing about *Get a Life* is that it really makes the
connections between faith and work, between Sunday morning
and Monday morning. It reflects Paul Valler's own experience
of a high-pressured life and this gives it plenty of true-to-life
wisdom.
Tim Chester, Author of Busy Christian's Guide to Busyness

Paul Valler has lived in the fast lane and understands how it feels.
He has written an honest and practical book born out of experience and avoiding quick-fit answers. If you truly seek shalom
(wholeness, peace and harmony) this book will help you find it.
Ian Coffey, Author and Speaker

As a full-time mother of three primary-aged children, a full-time
foster carer of two toddlers and a part-time writer, I constantly

have several plates spinning at once. In fact my life often seems to be a juggling of crises, deadlines, meetings, broken nights, hungry mouths and unfinished paperwork. It is a wonder I ever have time to read at all, let alone develop my relationship with God. But Paul Valler's book, far from adding to a 'to do' list, provides a helpful structure to re-evaluate life in the fast lane from a Christian perspective. With compelling case studies and wise insights, he inspires his readers to authenticate our work and worship by getting a life that is balanced, biblical and better equipped to handle all our daily dilemmas.

Miriam Kandiah, Full-time mother, Foster carer and Writer

This book is jam-packed with good advice and inspiring counsel for anyone, whether a new graduate in their first job, a mother juggling family and career responsibilities, the corporate executive at the top of the tree or the self-employed business woman working from home.

Get a Life is not just another book about faith and work. With its examination of purposes and identity, and the key importance of the choices we make, it seeks to put the whole of our lives – including our work – under God's scrutiny, so that we may live authentically for him.

Earthing what he says in Scripture, and posing useful insight questions at the end of each chapter, Paul Valler acts as a life coach encouraging the reader to consider his or her calling, and showing how to deal with practical issues such as avoiding burnout, changing jobs, guidance, accountability and speaking for Christ in the workplace.

Tricia Marnham, Speaker and former Solicitor

A versatile toolkit for those facing change.

Geoff Shattock, International Director of WorkTalk

Paul Valler deserves an immense 'well done' for his exposure of the flaws in many work-related ideas, the debilitating effect of peer pressure, the deceptive nature of workplace culture, e.g. 'having to stay late', and for nailing the artificial and often unhelpful sacred/secular divide.
Tom Stevens, Director of TransformWork UK

This is an easy read and yet the content is not shallow. It is perceptive and insightful, covering a huge amount of ground in a popular style . . . I particularly enjoyed the final part on personal mission which offers challenging insights on knowing God's purpose for our particular gifts and circumstances. The biblical basis for the author's thinking is lightly handled but always present to support the discussion.

This is an engaging read but if its true value is to be gained then it needs thoughtful reflection on the questions which conclude each section. Paul Valler gives the basis for making winning choices in life but it is up to the reader to think carefully, apply fully and make the bridge between the wider principles and the personal relevance.

A valuable book for individuals from all walks of life and a good resource for house group or cell discussion.
Dianne Tidball, Regional Minister East Midlands Baptist Association

This book is a practical, honest, Christ-centred help in our quest to live authentic lives.
Jago Wynne, All Souls, Workplace Ministry

Paul Valler

GET A LIFE

Winning choices for working people

ivp

Inter-Varsity Press
Norton Street, Nottingham NG7 3HR, England
Email: ivp@ivpbooks.com
Website: www.ivpbooks.com

First published 2008

British Library Cataloguing in Publication Data
A catalogue record for this book is available from the British Library.

ISBN: 978–1–84474–217–2

Set in Dante 12/15pt
Typeset in Great Britain by CRB Associates, Reepham, Norfolk
Printed and bound in Great Britain by Ashford Colour Press Ltd, Gosport, Hampshire

Inter-Varsity Press publishes Christian books that are true to the Bible and that communicate the gospel, develop discipleship and strengthen the church for its mission in the world.

Inter-Varsity Press is closely linked with the Universities and Colleges Christian Fellowship, a student movement connecting Christian Unions in universities and colleges throughout Great Britain, and a member movement of the International Fellowship of Evangelical Students. Website: www.uccf.org.uk

CONTENTS

SERIES PREFACE

A Time for Courage

Work matters hugely.

Work is the primary activity God created us to pursue – in communion with him and in partnership with others. Indeed, one of work's main goals is to make God's world a better place for all God's creatures to flourish in – to his glory

Yes, work matters hugely.

And to many people it brings the joys of purpose shared, relationships deepened, talents honed, character shaped, obstacles overcome, products made, people served and money earned – even amid the inevitable frustrations, failures and disagreements of working life in even the best of organizations.

Yes, work matters hugely. And so it matters hugely that for many people, most people actually, work is not only getting harder, longer, less satisfying and more draining, but is stretching its voracious tentacles into almost every area of life, sucking out the zing and whoosh and ease from time with family, friends, hobbies and community activities. UK citizens, for example, work four hours longer per person per week than the citizens of any other EU nation. We live in Slave New World.

How do we follow Jesus faithfully and fruitfully in such conditions?

Is coping – getting through the week – the height of our ambition? Surely not. But do we have good news for the workplace? Not just a truth to proclaim but a way to follow. Not just a way to follow but life, divine life, to infuse the quality of our work, the quality of our relationships at work, and the quality of our contribution to the culture of the organizations in which we work? In our current context, we not only need biblical insight and divine empowerment, but also courage to make tough decisions *about* work and life, and courage to make tough decisions *at* work.

That's what the Faith at Work series is designed to do: take on the tough issues facing workers and offer material that's fresh, either because it brings new insights to familiar topics or because the author's particular background and experience open up enlightening vistas. We've also tried to write the books so that there's something nutritious and tasty, not only for the leisurely diner, but also for the snacker snatching a quick read on a train, or in a break, or indeed, at the end of a demanding day.

The Lord be with you as you read. And the Lord be with you as you seek to follow him faithfully and courageously in your workplace.

Mark Greene
Series Editor
London Institute for Contemporary Christianity
2008

Commissioned volumes include:
What Does God Do on Monday? Ian Coffey
Working Models for our Time Mark Greene

ACKNOWLEDGMENTS

This book would not have been written without the sponsorship and encouragement of Mark Greene, who has been an inspirational mentor for me in the creative process, a kind editor and overall a jolly nice friend. Our habit of holding almost entire conversations in an Inspector Clouseau voice has brightened my life considerably.

Being a writer's wife can be a lonely role, yet I have felt completely released, supported and loved by Helen. Unknowingly I married someone with editorial ability. After years in business and in public speaking where most of my notes were in bullet-point form, Helen's ability to coax me gently into writing whole sentences was invaluable! Our two sons, Matt and Dave, have also been a great help and encouragement to me.

Friends who have helped me create fictional scenarios, or reviewed material, or prayed for me, are: Daphne Clifton, Paul Davies, Tony Elvidge, Jim Gallagher, Alison Green, Stephanie Heald, Paul Lambert, Sarah Osborne, Dave Phillips, Rachel Roberts, Graham Robinson, Jacky Widdup and Jackie Wright. Ian and Julie Wilkins generously offered their home in Norfolk as somewhere quiet to write and that helped me enormously. My grateful thanks to you all.

Kate Byrom and the staff at IVP have been a pleasure to work with. Their encouragement, professionalism and wise corrections have made a huge, positive difference to this book. Thank you.

FOREWORD

Of axes and aspirins

Call it coincidence if you like.

It's 7.45 a.m. and over the last few days I've been mulling over the foreword for this book. It's half-term for my kids, so, unusually, the TV's on. GMTV are doing a piece on stress and there's a national expert in the studio. He looks relaxed in his jeans and his open-necked shirt and his long, stylishly untidy hair. Then he's asked for his number one piece of advice. 'Take exercise,' comes the reply.

It's a good piece of advice, but the mother with kids who's sitting next to him isn't entirely convinced that it's really going to help her at all. Indeed, like most of what's on offer in the world of stress and work-life management, it doesn't peel the skin off the onion, never mind get to its heart. Yes, getting off the tube one stop early and walking to the office helps a mite. I do it. Yes, hot milk before bed helps a bit. Occasionally, I do that too. Though I don't, in case you're wondering, have slippers or a nightcap with a bobble on it. Yes, according to the 'stressperts', buying a couple of plants to oxygenate the office helps a tad. I haven't done that, primarily because I don't have a window and they'd die. Still, most of these little tips remind me of the man who walked into his doctor's surgery with an axe in his head, complained of a headache, and was given an aspirin. The aspirin may have helped a smidgen, but the axe is still in his head.

This books deals with the axe.

It isn't about managing stress, though it will help. It's about finding a way to flourish in a world that is fast paced, makes lots of demands and offers lots of options. And it approaches the topic by dealing with the causes of our difficulties, not the symptoms. It goes to the heart of the onion – asking us to examine our sense of purpose, or lack of it, to reflect on our identity, who we really are, and then to examine whether our priorities line up with our purpose and our identity. Simple? Yes. Radical? Yes. Easy? No. But it's probably the only way that's likely to make a lasting difference.

I've known Paul Valler for quite a few years now. Yes, he's been in a big job in a big company (finance and human resources director of Hewlett Packard Ltd) with a complex schedule, a wife, two growing children and church responsibilities. And that means he knows what it's like to have an axe in his head, how to get it out and how to deflect other axes.

Paul has certainly learned from personal experience, but this is no self-regarding 'do it my way' tract. Rather, Paul's insights have been reached by reflecting on the Word of God, on the life of Christ, on his own experience and on the work he's done with others, individually and in group seminars, over the last five years.

Paul has helped people. Paul does help people. He's not a pastor, but he has a genuine concern for people and a pastor's yearning to help people make the kind of wise choices that lead to more satisfying, adventurous, purposeful lives. This heartfelt, wise and vigorous book has the potential to help its readers do exactly what it says on the cover.

May it be so for you.

Mark Greene
LICC

1. INTRODUCTION – IS THIS YOUR LIFE?

One year stands out in my memory. I had just begun a very demanding job that required a lot of attention. I was usually working ten hours a day, and that did not include overseas business trips which frequently took me away from home. That same year my brother was diagnosed with a fatal brain tumour and both he and my parents needed support. Our teenage sons were in that phase of their launch into adult life that NASA refers to as 'maximum aerodynamic stress'. At the same time our church was struggling without a pastor and I was church secretary in pole position for sorting it out. My wife told me I was distant. Even when I was physically present at home, I was emotionally absent. Work-life balance problems? I've been there.

Still, my French boss did speak exactly like Inspector Clouseau, which provided occasional light relief. Clouseau usually leaves a trail of destruction and, looking back, I realize I made a mess of the situation in many ways. By God's grace I came through with my marriage and family intact, but there were long-term health and relationship consequences of being under that kind of sustained pressure. I wish I had not had to learn to 'get a life' the hard way.

Most talk about work-life balance focuses on time, but much more is hidden beneath the surface. Nine tenths of the iceberg of work-life pressure is a hidden reality we rarely want to face or talk about.

Tired, trapped and troubled

We are tired – not just because of working hours and travel. We are tired from being electronically connected to an always-on world, tired of people's expectations, and tired from the slavery of meeting targets. Many of us toil in sleep-deprived, energy-sapping workplaces of continuous intensity. We may not want to admit it, but we are far too tired – and our families and friends often get the dregs of lives worn out by work.

Sometimes we feel trapped: stuck in jobs that may not suit us, doing time in organizations where our development may seem ignored or blocked, and angry inside at the long-hours culture. Financial anxiety is the padlock keeping us there. We may also feel ethically compromised in work relationships and situations where there seems no right way out.

So instead of being at peace, we are troubled. We are unsettled by the different faces we have to present to different people and heavy hearted in some relationships that may not be working out well. Sometimes we wonder if we are really making a difference and feel uncertain about whether we are in God's will. We feel troubled by the strain on our health and sense of well-being and about what the long-term legacy of our life will be.

This is not another *Little Book of Calm* for the superficial treatment of these symptoms. Restful sounds of nature being piped over the intercom and screensavers with pictures of South Sea islands didn't do it for me. I needed more than lavender under the pillow and encouragement from a personal fitness trainer. Coping mechanisms were not enough. I needed help to understand and deal with the deep causes of work-life problems. So I went looking for something.

Identity, purpose and choices

My personal journey included decisions like refusing to re-locate for a promotion, working part time as finance director of a large company and changing career – choices that

2. GO AWAY, I'M BUSY

Pressure Pressure Pressure

Jack ran down the stairs and out the front door. With a passing twinge of guilt over his failure to repair the sticking latch, he slammed the door shut and jumped in the car. Then he remembered his laptop. Muttering an apology to God for what he had just said, he charged back inside, grabbed the bag and slammed the door again. 'What are you doing?' called Liz, but there was no reply.

Jack was late. He was often late. Driving away, he punched his mobile for voicemail and heard the words, 'You have nine messages.'

'What? Unbelievable! It's only a quarter to eight.' He blew out a long sigh as he joined the inevitable queue.

'Hey Jack, hope you're well. Can we have ten minutes today to finalize the position before our customer meeting tomorrow? Best time for me would be end of play – I'm pretty full with back-to-back meetings otherwise. Let me know. Cheers.'

'Yeah, of course I'd like to be late back from work as well,' said Jack sarcastically. The queue started moving.

'Next message.' The voice was older and slower. 'Oh, hello Jack, sorry I missed you after the service. I was wondering if you would like to have lunch together sometime this week and chat through the agenda for Thursday night. Are you free today? I'm at home, so just call to let me know. God bless.'

Jack gave a little snort. 'Lunch! What planet are you on?'

He finished listening to all nine messages, only to have the system announce, 'You have one new message.'

'Leave me alone!' he shouted.

It was Liz. 'Hi, it's me. The front door won't shut. Can you tell me what to do?'

Shaking his head, he dialled home. He felt trapped by his responsibilities, burdened with all his obligations and intimidated by other people's expectations. After calling Liz, he stared ahead, cruising in the outside lane, trying to relax. Pressure at work, pressure at home and pressure at church, a seemingly eternal triangle. 'I just need a break,' he thought.

The rush-hour traffic slowed again under the flyover. As his queue crawled past three giant pillars, the graffiti on them revealed itself one word at a time, and Jack gripped the wheel as the message struck home. *Good . . . Morning . . . Lemmings.* 'God help me,' he said.

There is something about journeys that creates an opportunity for reflection. They are 'in-between times' when we can suddenly realize something significant – a flash of insight in a humdrum moment. Perhaps you are reading this on a journey or during another kind of 'in-between time'.

Our lives are often lived at such a pace that it is only in these momentary pauses that we really start to think. Then our problem is that we are back into the race before we have had a chance to work out what to do. Even when the same thought occurs to us more than once, it can so easily get lost in the busy atmosphere around us.

The Bible warns about this issue of realizing something, but not applying it.

Those who listen to the word but do not do what it says are like people who look at their faces in a mirror and, after looking at themselves, go away and immediately forget what they look like.

(James 1:23–24 NIVI)

For change to take place, insight has to be captured and then turned into action. Without that there can be no progress. If we allow our insights to slip away into the back of our mind, we fail to learn and grow.

Too much to do

After a heavy day Jack was once again late leaving work, silently grateful for the fact that the graffiti artists had only written on one side of the pillars. He felt drained and tried to psych himself up for 're-entry' at home. He knew Liz would be at her low point after three hours of post-school activities, feeding the kids and keeping them in order. Then he groaned as he remembered he'd agreed to cover for Matt at the youth group.

As the traffic stopped again he shut his eyes, only to open them later to find he had a thirty-yard gap in front of him. Embarrassed, he jabbed the accelerator . . . stalled . . . then tried to ignore the shaking heads overtaking his car. 'I'm living in survival mode,' he thought. 'What can I stop doing? Everything I do is important. I'm on the proverbial treadmill and I want to get off.'

Jack saw the people in his work and life like spinning plates on poles. If he didn't keep up the spinning, one of them would fall and smash: his boss, his clients, his wife, his kids, his health, his role at church . . . How could he ignore any of them? He didn't *want* to ignore any of them.

What can Jack do? Rushing between things, he is trying to be all things to everyone and burning out in the process. The same feelings apply whether we are a male thirty-something professional or a mum trying to juggle a job and childcare. Whatever our age or lifestyle, everyone experiences competing pressures and feels like a plate-spinner sometimes.

We can even enjoy this kind of busyness and feel good about our productivity – I certainly did for a while. Then we start to realize that our pattern of behaviour is becoming damaging – more damaging than we want to admit. Our relationships become strained and we begin to feel an uneasy sense of being pulled apart as we try to cope with all the different roles and expectations. Psychologists call it 'fragmentation'.

Jack's problem is that he lacks any guiding principles that might enable him to say 'no' to something. Whilst desperately needing to set boundaries, he does not know how to deal with the tension he would feel and the disappointment of others. So, without that ability to say 'no' in a way others can accept, he lives in slavery to everyone else's expectations.

Insight Capture Questions
1. Where do I feel pulled in many directions? What 'plates' am I spinning?
2. Where do I feel I cannot say 'no'? Why?

3. WISDOM FOR THE WAY

Wisdom is supreme; therefore get wisdom.

Though it cost all you have, get understanding.

(Proverbs 4:7)

Difficult choices

The waitress stood with a tray of nibbles – neatly spiralled parcels of bread and smoked salmon. Andrew liked salmon, but he had gluten intolerance and knew the bread would disagree with him. So, reluctantly, he refused. It seemed to have been a day of saying 'no'. He had refused a promotion to Geneva that would have brought him more money and status. His boss was surprised at his choice and annoyed that his recommendation of Andrew had been undermined by the person he thought would be most pleased. Then Andrew had refused to attend the special church meeting tonight and disappointed his minister. Perhaps the most difficult moment had been telling his wife he would not be around on Friday evening for the party.

Andrew did not like saying 'no', but he had learned an important lesson. Saying 'yes' to someone often involves saying 'no' to someone else. Andrew had said 'yes' to keeping his family in this local community and church, and that meant 'no' to Geneva. He had said 'yes' to attending his daughter's prize-giving evening with its inedible nibbles, and that meant 'no' to a special church meeting. He had said 'yes' to supporting his work colleagues in committing to an important dinner, and that meant 'no' to a party. As a result of these choices he suffered incredulity, disappointment and irritation from people he cared about.

Their reactions showed that Andrew still lacked the ability to communicate his choices in a way that helped others understand. Yet they respected him – some even envied him. Andrew was one of those people who seemed to have 'got it together'.

What is the secret that enables Andrew to rise above being a victim of pressure to become a wise chooser of priorities? Why is Jack not as far forward in this area as Andrew?

Part of the answer lies in understanding a pattern of human behaviour older than the Bible. In ancient cultures the deities were thought of as dreaded forces arrayed against humans. The gods were divided against each other and could cause people to be divided within themselves as they tried to appease more than one. People were afraid to worship only one god for fear of being punished by those they had rejected. So they resorted to polytheism – the worship of many gods (see Judges 2:12).

The same thing is happening today. Our priorities can become like little 'gods'. Clifford Elliott points out in his excellent book *With Integrity of Heart* that most of us have become practising polytheists. We are under the tyranny of too many priorities, gods who will not share our devotion with other gods, gods who demand all of us. We worship one god in one situation and another god in another situation.

Perhaps very occasionally we may meet someone like Andrew who seems to have 'got it all together'. It is not that their circumstances are easier than ours, but there seems to be a quiet clarity about their lives that is noticeable. What gives a person that kind of simplicity and peace?

It has something to do with understanding and choosing our values. Our lives become oriented around whatever or whoever we value most – whatever we choose to worship. All kinds of potential idols compete for our attention and devotion: money, work, property, status, popularity, sex, our children, another person, our self-interests – the list is endless. If we allow any of these 'gods' to become too important, our lives become distorted as we try to serve whatever we have elevated above its place.

Things fall into the right perspective and our life becomes more integrated when we recognize and stay focused on the true and living God. As Rick Warren says, 'If you want to know why you were placed on this planet, you must begin with God. You were made by God and for God – and until you understand that, life will never make sense.' All our other 'gods' must take their proper place under the Lord God Almighty. 'The fear of the LORD is the beginning of wisdom' (Proverbs 9:10).

Making the right choices depends on being clear about our values. To develop authenticity and integrity – by which I mean consistently living our values – we must develop clarity and conviction. Andrew had developed sufficient personal conviction to influence his responses to the pressures and expectations of others. He was free from trying to placate the various 'gods' demanding his attention.

In the life of Jesus, we see him making decisions on the basis of inner conviction. For example, at the height of a period when he was healing many people, everyone was pressurizing him to stick around in one town. It would have been a very good thing to do exactly that. Perhaps anticipating the pressure, Jesus took time out early in the morning to pray and then said very clearly, 'Let us go somewhere else – to the nearby villages – so that I can preach there also. That is why I have come' (Mark 1:38). He had developed a simple and powerful conviction about what he was meant to do next, about the right choice.

Developing clear personal convictions about the choices we face in work and life is something to aim for, and it is something that, as Christians, we do not have to do on our own. God can work through our thoughts and perceptions with a divine affirmation. The more we have renewed our minds through Scripture, the more we have sought God in prayer, the more we experience God in the community of his people, then the clearer our convictions can become.

This process is not infallible. Interference from our thoughts, emotions and outward circumstances can be confusing. That is why it is wise to check our conclusions with the Bible and with others. For a Christian genuinely seeking God's will, the journey of thought and prayer can reach a point of conviction where there is a deep inner peace. 'Let the peace of Christ rule in your hearts' (Colossians 3:15).

It has been my experience that this kind of inner resonance is possible in making work and life decisions. The principles shared in this book are the result of that process in my own life. My prayer is that they will help to inspire you to make the right choices.

Insight Capture Questions
1. Who or what are the priorities in my life?
2. Which of these have I made too important?

PART 1

LIVING AUTHENTICALLY

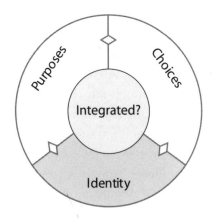

Figure 2

If you wish to communicate,
    on this one thing, please meditate:
Avoid pretence, be real, be true,
    that I might know who's really you.
Show me your self in honesty,
    and not the you you'd have me see.
We will not progress very far,
    unless you show me who you are.
Yet all is lost, if you don't see
    the person who is really me!
(Gill Rowell, *The Spiritual @dventures of CyberCindy*)

4. WHO DO YOU THINK YOU ARE?

The Spirit himself testifies with our spirit that we are God's children.
(Romans 8:16)

What is it that defines your identity? What do you say if someone asks you to introduce yourself? You probably give your name, maybe something about your family or where you live, and perhaps a job title or organizational role you have. We all do this and what we are doing is giving a series of labels which help others 'position' and remember us. Yet rarely do we share what makes up our real identity – the quality and depth of our personal relationships and beliefs. To really know someone else involves understanding these deeply personal things. To know myself means knowing which of my relationships and beliefs are most important. To know who you are, you must know *whose* you are.

This is a much deeper issue than most people realize. Christians have a key relationship that transforms identity – our relationship with God through Christ. The potential impact of it is greatly underestimated by most of us. Mere intellectual acceptance that our identity is in Christ is quite different from experiencing the personal application of that truth. The song about the ugly duckling that grew into a beautiful swan is a classic example. Until the swan realized it was a swan, it continued to behave on the basis of an out-of-date identity. When the realization struck home, it changed everything. In the same way, knowing who we are in Christ is a powerful reality. It changes not only how we see ourselves, but also how we see the world and make choices.

Take the issue of working long hours. Sometimes it may be genuinely necessary to work late, but many workplaces simply have a culture of staying late and that culture creates peer pressure. Workplaces like this promote the ideas that your self-worth depends on your ability to perform and your acceptance depends on your willingness to conform. Those ideas are flawed, and their power is neutralized by the truth that your self-worth and acceptance are ultimately found in who you are as God's child. When we really know that truth, it sets us free and we become less driven by culture and peer pressure. Deceptions like 'having to stay late' have less influence as our motivations spring from a strong sense of identity and self-worth in Christ. We are in the world, but not of the world.

Think about how the system in which we live promotes the idea that our identity is based on what we can achieve. The education system awards grades. Sports personalities are built on breaking records. Promotion to bigger job titles is based on success and achievement. How easily we believe the lie that we are what we do.

Bored and bothered

Stella put down her coffee, slumped onto the sofa and stared at the mess. Birthday toys were strewn over the floor and a half-eaten biscuit was decaying on the carpet. After lunch was the time her toddler went to sleep for a while. She felt bored and restless. A recurrent thought troubled her: 'I'm just not cut out for this, my brain is going.'

Stella used to be an actuary. Using a calculator is not usually thought of as exciting work, but right now being a mum was a lot less exciting than being an actuary. After the first few months of motherhood, she had begun to feel increasingly frustrated. Stella had gone from being a respected professional to 'Johnnie's mum'. She agonized over the possibility of returning to work, but guilt held her back. Tormented by a feeling of unfulfilled potential, yet afraid of leaving her son with a childminder, she did not know what to do. Yesterday her husband had said, 'Look Stella, I don't want you to go crazy with boredom. There's nothing wrong with being a working mother. Just go for it.' She had nodded and smiled.

After another brief moment of self-doubt, Stella picked up the phone and called her old boss. She had to leave a message, but an hour later the phone rang while she was clearing up. 'Stella! Great to hear from you! Desperate to come back yet?'

'Yes,' said Stella simply.

'Good,' he said. 'Come in and have a chat tomorrow.' The juggling was about to start.

Stella was beginning what Nancy Kremen Bolton calls 'The Third Shift', which applies particularly to working mothers. At work (the first shift) working mothers worry about their children and home. At home (the second shift) they are concerned about work. Feelings of freedom and empowerment can alternate with feelings of guilt and failure. The third shift is the emotional and mental energy drain that goes on all the time. The third shift is the 24-hour-a-day nagging doubt that you might not be doing the thing you ought to be doing. It is a debilitating worry that creates confusion about who we are, or should be, or will be.

We have a tendency to think like the world and define ourselves by what we do. So when our role changes, we may feel our identity has also changed. Going from actuary to mum feels like an identity loss. Then going from full-time mum back to actuary feels like an identity compromise. Every time there is a change in our role we feel destabilized, because we have allowed our identity to be defined by what we do. Identity and role confusion is only part of the many challenges of being a working mum, but it is one that seems to be a common experience.

Drifting

Mark lazily made his third cup of coffee that day. He had solved the puzzle, browsed the internet and been for a walk. Being unemployed was unbearable. A deep feeling of unease gnawed away at him. It wasn't just the fear of not being able to provide, it was a feeling of pointlessness – a vague feeling of guilt and depression, of being unwanted and useless. What made it worse was the silent pressure of his family. He knew they were sympathetic. Jill didn't say much about it, but whenever she asked how things were going Mark felt under huge pressure. He knew she was walking on eggshells, but he still felt criticized before she said anything. Mark flitted between tetchiness, denial and gloom. He didn't talk much.

For the first week or two he had been concerned, but still energized, optimistic and expectant. Maybe he was a little naïve, but he still felt he had an identity from his previous job and organization. Since that connection had expired and he hadn't managed to secure another one, he felt his identity adrift, his legitimacy gone. He wasn't so sure of himself. It was harder to look people in the eye. His self-esteem had been knocked and he had only been off work for a couple of months!

Leaving work can be an enormous shock. People often feel very disoriented when they leave paid employment, because they feel a major part of life with meaning and identity has ended. When Stella left to have a baby and Mark lost his job, they both felt they had lost their identity.

Everyone needs a sense of acceptance, belonging and self-worth. Those needs were in humankind at creation, and were satisfied in the context of a loving relationship with God. The Bible explains that when humankind chose independence we lost our relationship with God. The security of loving acceptance and belonging was replaced by separation and a feeling of rejection. Innocence was replaced by feelings of guilt and shame. This is what characterizes a 'failure identity' that is evident amongst so many people today.

The good news of the gospel is that God has restored our relationship with him by reconciling us to himself through the death and resurrection of Christ on our behalf. Christians are like the prodigal son who went his own way, but, realizing his emptiness, was drawn back to the father. The prodigal's return is a poignant story of identity being re-established. His father gives him a robe, a ring and sandals on his feet – symbols of sonship and a restored relationship. In the same way, those who turn to God and ask for forgiveness are adopted as his children. 'How great is the love the Father has lavished on us, that we should be called children of God! And that is what we are!' (1 John 3:1)

Have you ever considered that your work might be deceiving you about your real identity? Devotion to work can subtly and gradually reposition your sense of who you are to become entirely job based. At the extreme, this is what happens when people become workaholics. The job becomes the be-all and end-all. The role and status, reward and recognition become addictive. No wonder pay is sometimes called compensation! It may be the only compensation you get for losing the rest of your life.

Organizations and jobs offer an identity, because they offer roles and responsibilities with a sense of belonging and purpose – reinforced by job titles, name badges with logos and business cards. People feel more secure with these things, transient though they are. If we let our identity be defined by them, a deep deception enters our thinking like a geological fault line. Then a change in job title can be like a psychological earthquake, as everything we built on the previous identity collapses.

Our relationship to God does not alter by losing or gaining a job. Everyone experiences some difficulty with change, but if our identity is rooted in Christ instead of our role, change becomes less threatening. When we are secure about being in Christ, we are better placed to make changes and respond to changes in work and life.

Insight Capture Questions
1. How different is the way I introduce myself at work from the way I introduce myself socially?
2. How much of my identity is tied up with my job?

5. AFRAID OR AUTHENTIC?

It is for freedom that Christ has set us free.
(Galatians 5:1)

Afraid

Extracts from cynical Dilbert cartoons were pinned to the noticeboard in the coffee area where Linda was making her first drink of the day. Recent job losses meant that motivational meltdown had struck in less than a week. Even the smell of the air conditioning felt threatening. The atmosphere tensed as Brad walked quietly down the open office corridor. Everyone focused on their screens to hide their anxiety.

Brad had his own anxiety. After having to make two people redundant, he was heading for the top floor wondering whether his own job was on the line. His boss was a difficult man who ruled by creating a climate of fear. Fear of disapproval, fear of being thought incompetent and, ultimately, the fear of being fired plagued all his staff. No-one knew it, but as Brad walked past Linda he started praying silently.

Linda didn't know Brad was a Christian. She thought he was a fair manager, but knew nothing of his faith. She had been in his group for six months and never realized his commitment to Christ, even though she sometimes prayed for him. Brad suspected she was a believer, but he'd never asked. Such things were just not talked about at work.

Why are we sometimes reluctant to be open about our Christian identity in the place we spend most of our waking lives? The answer to a greater or lesser extent is fear. We fear being socially awkward or violating some unwritten rule. We fear rejection or being persecuted in some way. It is fear that masks my authenticity, demanding that I conceal the real me. It was fear that caused the apostle Peter to try to hide his identity when he felt under pressure; fear that made him deny Jesus.

The accusation to Peter in the courtyard was, 'Surely you are one of them, for you are a Galilean' (Mark 14:70). It was not about his cultural identity or a Galilean ID card. What was really being challenged was his personal identity as defined by his relationships. 'You are one of them' (a follower of Jesus) was the accusation. It was his committed relationship that forged his personal identity. Since the key relationship for a Christian is with God through faith in Christ, it is the Spirit within us that anchors our identity. 'The Spirit himself testifies with our spirit that we are God's children' (Romans 8:16).

Suppressing our Christian identity is like trying to keep an inflated ball under water. Eventually it becomes impossible. Either the ball surfaces, or we have to deflate it. That is what happens if we continually try to suppress who we really are. If our true identity surfaces after a long time, then the people we know feel betrayed. If it deflates, then we feel we have betrayed ourselves.

The crying need is for authenticity. Viv Thomas says,

Having to adapt yourself to many audiences can break your life into a series of disconnected fragments which never seem to come together. Sometimes we choose to live with a split and shattered self and hope that somehow neither we nor others will notice. We hide from ourselves and do all we can to avoid one part of our lives fully encountering the other.

The pressure to mask ourselves in different settings is subtle and strong. We want to be accepted and approved by everyone. Without realizing it, Christians can end up behaving like different people in different situations. Losing our internal integrity like this is the greatest stress of all, far more harmful to us than competition or pressure. After Peter had denied Jesus, 'he went outside and wept bitterly' (Luke 22:62).

If we fear rejection, we put the approval of others above the approval of God. This is how Saul behaved. The people had asked for a king, and the people were ultimately whom he followed. 'I was afraid of the people and so I gave in to them' (1 Samuel 15:24). Saul derived his identity primarily from being popular. His life was a search for external validation. Whatever the people wanted, Saul did, even when it went against what God said. Ultimately he lost his identity as king.

David, however, derived his identity primarily from his personal relationship with God. We can see this in his prayers and psalms (1 Chronicles 29:10–20), where his emotional expression shows how close he was to God. He looked at things through God's perspective. Although he had many relationships that were important, his over-riding primary allegiance was to God and he was known as a man after God's own heart (1 Samuel 13:14).

In the workplace we are socially accustomed to a gradual disclosure as we get to know people. So as working relationships develop, it becomes increasingly false and odd not to share who we really are. Yet working culture often hinders this kind of honesty. In today's world, separating your personal beliefs from your working relationships is regarded as desirable and necessary for avoiding clashes with customers, colleagues and regulators. Policies aimed at encouraging inclusiveness can lead to a sterile avoidance of anything that seems religious. Political correctness is a climate that deadens the authentic expression of personality and suppresses the expression of belief. This is where Christians can be tempted to hide.

Work is assumed to be an activity necessary to earn your living and Christianity is assumed to be your private, 'leisure time' activity – a belief system that applies to your personal life and not to your work life. It is called the sacred/secular divide. Ironically, the church unwittingly encourages this divide. People like Brad regularly go to church, but often find very little that is relevant to their issues at work. So just as we do not talk about our Christianity at work, we rarely talk about our work in church.

This sacred/secular divide impacts our personal identity. We can compartmentalize ourselves and present a different face to the workplace from the one we present to the rest of our church or family. We can experience a personal sacred/secular divide, marginalizing our faith to only a part of our lives. Is this your experience? Is Christ in you visible in one part of your life and unrecognizable in another part?

Integrating work and life means smashing the sacred/secular divide in our lives – seeing the reality of Colossians 3:23:

> Whatever you do, work at it with all your heart, as working for the Lord, not for human masters, since you know that you will receive an inheritance from the Lord as a reward. It is the Lord Christ you are serving. (NIVI)

Ultimately we serve him in everything we do. There is no sacred/secular divide in the kingdom of God.

Choosing to believe that my identity is first and foremost in Christ is like the moment when the conductor of an orchestra asks the oboist to sound an A. At first there is just noise as all the musicians try to align themselves with that note. Then, as everyone converges towards it, the noise diminishes. When they all finally sound together, there is a moment of homecoming and rest. Somewhere deep inside me there is a resonance that is Christ alone. I want to know that sound and daily tune my life to it.

One of the lovely things about children is that they have not yet learned to 'manage their faces'. You can see what a child is feeling just by looking at them. They really do live with 'unveiled faces' (2 Corinthians 3:18), with complete authenticity and no mask. Jesus was like that. He never veiled his face. He had perfect emotional intelligence, but he never had a mask. When we live open and authentic lives, our Christian identity will be revealed when we show compassion and kindness and speak graciously, or when we set boundaries and resist evil. Opportunities for all these things arise regularly in the workplace, in the home and in the community. The distinctive difference of Christ will soon make itself evident if we do not suppress him.

Seek to get a better understanding of who you are in Christ and live with an authentic, open and consistent Christian identity for better work-life integration. Our choice at work, at home and at church is to believe what God says about who we are and then to live with an unveiled face, being real with people about who we are and about our key relationships. When we develop this kind of integrity, we experience less internal stress and greater freedom.

Insight Capture Questions
1. Am I known as a Christian amongst my work colleagues?
2. What might I be hiding about myself?

6. CONNECTED IN COMMUNITY

> You also, like living stones, are being built into a spiritual
> house . . .
> (1 Peter 2:5)

Our Christian identity lies at the heart of three key relationships. The first is with God, from whom our new identity is
derived. The second is with our Christian community, in
which our identity is nurtured. The third is in the world,
where our identity is expressed, challenged and tested. When
these three relationships are all healthy, our lives are healthy
and God's mission in the world is being advanced.

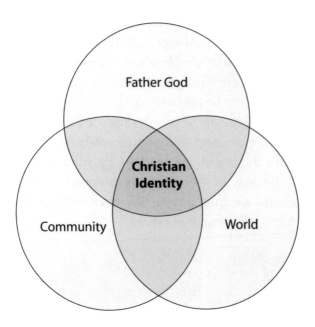

Figure 3. Key relationships for integration

This relational framework is an important way to think and it underpins the thinking in this book. Christianity is a relational religion. 'Now this is eternal life: that they may know you, the only true God, and Jesus Christ, whom you have sent' (John 17:3).

The Bible describes the fall of humankind as a rupture in relationship with God and the cross as a reconciliation – a relational term. The Trinity itself is a community where each person values the others and Jesus' desire is for community:

> I pray also for those who will believe in me through their
> message, that all of them may be one, Father, just as you are
> in me and I am in you.
> (John 17:20–21)

Understanding work and life through a relational lens is consistent with the way God sees it. At the end of my life I am going to remember the people who matter to me. Relationship and community are what give our lives meaning.

No-one else can be the father or the mother to your child, or the husband or wife to your spouse, or the son or daughter or brother or sister that you are. Whatever you do at work or in the world can be done by someone else, but no-one else can be you in your personal relationships. Relationships are truly unique. We discover our role in life through our relationship to others.

Slipping

Two men in hard hats were arguing as he entered the Portakabin. Swear words sprayed like machine-gun bullets from their mouths – the culture of the construction industry was expletives for everything. Carlos was used to it. The thing that did embarrass him in the struggle for the language was when an occasional English swear word came from his own lips.

His partner had left him after he had become a Christian and he felt it best to move away. Carlos had contacts in the construction industry and had made a new life for himself. He was doing well, but missed the friendship and support of the people back home in the church. He was beginning to find it difficult to keep up his new faith and felt himself slipping back into old habits.

Like Carlos, we may be surrounded by behaviours that grate, morality that undermines us and media messages that sow doubt in our minds. An individual Christian who tries to live in the world of work without belonging to a Christian community is like someone trying to balance on a two-legged stool. The community of believers is the missing leg that supports and stabilizes our ability to engage with the world as people of faith. We need that supportive community as an essential component of an integrated work-life.

Choosing to belong to a Christian community is a strategic decision for several reasons:

1. God has chosen the church as his channel of communication in the world. 'His intent was that now, through the church, the manifold wisdom of God should be made known . . . ' (Ephesians 3:10) Belonging makes you better connected with God's mission.

2. A Christian community keeps our attention on Christ and his Word, which strengthens our faith: ' . . . and you will do well to pay attention to it, as to a light shining in a dark place . . . ' (2 Peter 1:19); 'We must pay more careful attention, therefore, to what we have heard, so that we do not drift away' (Hebrews 2:1).

3. We are not strong enough to handle spiritual opposition on our own. If we are to avoid becoming dry, complacent and ultimately neutralized as a distinctive force for God in the world, we need the community of believers. 'With this in mind, be alert and always keep on praying for all the saints' (Ephesians 6:18).

4. Being in community has the effect of developing our character and motivating us into service. 'And let us consider how we may spur one another on towards love and good deeds. Let us not give up meeting together, as some are in the habit of doing, but let us encourage one another – and all the more as you see the Day approaching' (Hebrews 10:24–25).

Belonging to a Christian community is a very different experience from belonging to a work community. Workplace relationships are based on getting the job done, but relationships in the body of Christ are based on a common identity in Christ. Work culture is performance based and workplaces encourage achievements, whereas Christian culture is grace based and communities encourage people. Workplaces are often places with high levels of insecurity and where trust is shallow. Christian communities, though they are flawed and sometimes fail, have a much greater sense of stability and mutual support. Belonging to a local Christian community anchors and nurtures our core life principles in a way that workplace groups cannot do.

Recently I spoke to a Christian from Africa who is on an engineering assignment in the UK as part of a multinational company. I asked him when he moved here, in which of the two communities he felt most quickly integrated – his new workplace or his new local church. Despite the fact that he already worked for the organization that brought him here, he unhesitatingly chose the church, because he felt that his personal values and life principles matched with the Christian community. Though significant differences exist between the styles of church in Africa and the UK, they did not prevent his sense of belonging here.

A common problem is that our workplace is often geographically distant from our Christian community. Business is global, but people are local. At work we may find ourselves not only distant, but also out of rhythm with the local patterns that help to stabilize our lives. I spoke to some Christian journalists who told me that being a reporter can sometimes be 'a life with no rhythm', except the editorial deadline. Work commitments like that can make it difficult to integrate into any community. Since regular rhythms are healthy, this is where we need to be both assertive in maintaining boundaries on our work and creative in finding new ways of being in Christian community.

One way to address the issue is to find some Christian community at or near your workplace. A group of Christians made 'Train Church' famous by agreeing to travel together from the south coast en route to their work in London. They 'did life together' on the train. Another example in the City of London is the practice of 'Workplace Bands' – small groups of Christians who share the same workplace. A Band meets together on site immediately before work over coffee, or occasionally over lunch. The agenda is to acknowledge Christ's presence, share the pressures and pray together, both supporting each other and pursuing the purpose of God in that workplace.

Taking this kind of initiative to find and create ways to be regularly connected to other Christians is an important principle. Workplace networks are not a substitute for local church, but they can strengthen our faith and our impact.

Insight Capture Questions
1. How well am I connected to a Christian community?
2. What could I do to deepen my experience of Christian community?

7. BETTER TO BELONG

It is not good for the man to be alone.
(Genesis 2:18)

Surprise surprise

Brad had guessed it was coming and now he actually felt relieved. The prospect of no more Monday meetings was bliss. He collected his stuff and looked round one last time. Driving home slowly, he felt grateful for family and grateful for church. It was at a time like this that he was glad he had friends who cared about him and would pray for him.

Brad's experience started him thinking about how he could make a difference by supporting other men in their work. Initially unsure how his suggestion would be received, he was bowled over by the interest shown in his offer to pray for the relationships between each man and his boss. In the days ahead, Brad became something of a confidant. He had found an unmet need and occasionally dropped in for lunch at the workplaces of his friends to meet and pray with them. It took him four months to secure another position, and afterwards he was able to help others going through the emotional turmoil of job change.

Mutual support is lacking for many people at work today. The economically developed world, with its focus on the individual and on the consumer, has largely lost the ability to give and receive help. A Christian community is a place where that can and does happen regularly, creating a healthy environment of cooperation. People are able to contribute by using their abilities and gifts and this develops individuals as well as strengthening the whole body.

Christian communities are at their best when they actively support their members in the wider world and workplace. By treating each person in the workplace like a missionary and praying for them, Brad extended Christian influence into the workplace in a deeper and more effective way. He understood that to make a difference, he had to connect with people in their everyday experience at work.

Working life involves stress, often underpinned by frustration and anger. Poor interpersonal skills in the management of people, the unfairness of pay differentials and lack of recognition are common. Righteous anger at injustice is understandable and, wisely and properly expressed, can carry weight. However, at the personal level, one of the most important life skills in this kind of environment is forgiveness. Individuals who have not learned how to forgive from the heart can easily become relationally disabled, either withdrawing into a shell, or behaving in ways that make others withdraw. This is a key reason for dysfunctional teams and weak organizations.

What we learn in the church can help us in the workplace. Living in Christian community is also not always easy. Relationships can become strained for various reasons and then we get the opportunity to practise receiving and giving forgiveness. It is an aspect of God's love that lies at the heart of our community of faith in Christ, who died that we could both experience forgiveness and release it. We have to learn to accept and forgive imperfection and failure in ourselves, in our colleagues and in our friends. Without forgiveness, the inevitable pain and disappointment we experience from others conquers us and our bitterness keeps us in bondage. With forgiveness there is freedom. Living in Christian community helps us face this truth and bring the reality of it into the world of work. It develops our capability to conduct relationships in an authentic and healthy way.

Belonging makes all the difference

She was breathing heavily, bruising easily and showing red marks on her skin. Suspecting meningitis, her parents took her to the emergency doctor and by late Saturday afternoon, childhood leukaemia was confirmed. She was just two and a half years old. Initial drug treatment for leukaemia at that age sometimes results in death.

At church the following morning, children and adults alike were praying for her in their groups. On Sunday evening the girl's father stayed with her in hospital to allow her mother and older sister to go home, together with grandparents, who had come to help. After a weary weekend they found a shepherd's pie by the front door. It was the beginning of practical support from the church, which organized lifts to and from hospital, meals and collecting the older sister from school when her mum could not meet her.

Unfortunately the little girl's condition deteriorated – she went into renal failure and her life hung by a thread. On Tuesday she was rushed 100 miles to an intensive care bed at the Bristol Children's Hospital. That Tuesday evening, a day of prayer and fasting concluded with the largest single prayer meeting ever held in the church, asking God to save the child's life. It was an emotional occasion – I was there.

At this little girl's dedication, the following verse had been prayed over her:

When you pass through the waters,
    I will be with you;
and when you pass through the rivers,
    they will not sweep over you.
When you walk through the fire,
    you will not be burned;
    the flames will not set you ablaze.
(Isaiah 43:2)

God answered the prayers of his people in the way they had longed for, and she lived.

Then followed the long haul of treatment for leukaemia, with regular trips to hospital and the inevitable string of infections and mini-crises. The church has continued to pray and offer practical and emotional help. When the family moved house, teams of volunteers cleaned the old house and helped put up their furniture in the new house. Sometimes, when the family are having a bad week, a chocolate cake makes a miraculous appearance. Living in community makes a big difference, not just to home life, but also to the ability to continue to hold down a job during a crisis.

Outside the family, I do not know of any other organization able to provide that kind of all-round local support, not only in a crisis, but also for the long haul. The local Christian community is unique. Of course it is also imperfect and does not always deliver as much love and care as Jesus would want. There is something especially motivating about a young child in danger and there may be other people reading this whose experiences have not been as positive as those of this family. Nevertheless, living in a community of faith still represents the best way to live.

Insight Capture Questions
1. How much prayer support do I have for my role at work?
2. What have I learned about myself from being in a Christian community?

8. EXILED AT WORK?

How can we sing the songs of the LORD
    while in a foreign land?
(Psalm 137:4)

Uncomfortable

Sunita ignored the wolf whistle and pressed her lips together as she walked out of the office to the car. 'Mind how you go, we drive on the left here, you know.' She closed her eyes and sighed as the door closed behind her. Thinly veiled sexual and racial jibes were a daily experience from the young men who dominated the estate agency in which she worked. The culture was all about money, with power a close second. The agents were competitive, mainly white and filled with testosterone. Already ostracized and left out of social occasions with 'the boys', Sunita felt lonely, abused and uncomfortable at work. She tried to minimize time in the office.

Sunita's client was another young woman, Amanda, a first-time buyer who was struggling to get on the property ladder. She was getting desperate, having already lost out twice to a higher bidder. Amanda had found out afterwards that her previous agent had delayed her offer to the vendor hoping for a higher bid. Bogus information about other offers had been passed to her and Amanda had understandably become more cynical. Sunita knew this was not going to be easy or lucrative. They spent an hour chatting over her requirements before parting with a promise to talk later that day.

Clients loved dealing with Sunita, but the team knew she had one fundamental flaw. She was honest. Unwilling to exaggerate or embellish the truth about properties or people, Sunita knew that the rest of the agents looked down on her as someone who settled for a second-rate result and earned less than they did in fees. That didn't matter to her until the agency introduced a group target and a bonus for group sales. Suddenly anybody who looked like a weak link was going to be expendable.

Over lunch in the car, Sunita prayed about the challenge she faced at work and asked God for help. Her Bible was open at Psalm 138.

> Though the LORD is on high, he looks upon the
>   lowly,
>   but the proud he knows from afar.
> Though I walk in the midst of trouble,
>   you preserve my life;
> you stretch out your hand against the anger of my
>   foes,
>   with your right hand you save me.
> The LORD will fulfil his purpose for me;
>   your love, O LORD, endures for ever –
>   do not abandon the works of your hands.
> (Psalm 138:6–8)

The cost of being open about who we really are can sometimes be rejection. Jesus experienced that. He was rejected at Nazareth (Matthew 6, 13; Luke 4). There are some workplaces where persecution of Christians is a sport. A friend of mine who works in a warehouse has to endure foul language simply because others know that it hurts. The Bible says that being identified as a Christian will bring difficulties: 'Dear friends, do not be surprised at the painful trial you are suffering, as though something strange were happening to you' (1 Peter 4:12). 'Everyone who wants to live a godly life in Christ Jesus will be persecuted' (2 Timothy 3:12). Accepting the different reactions of people to who we are is something we have to learn. That takes a lot of forgiveness.

Some workplaces feel like an exile for Christians. Scripture says of the people of faith that 'they admitted that they were aliens and strangers on earth' (Hebrews 11:13). Organizations may have laudable public values, but many have a working culture that is indifferent to God and driven by personal agendas and ambition. Christians can feel that they are in Jerusalem on Sunday and Babylon on Monday, asking the question, 'How can we sing the songs of the Lord while in a foreign land?' (Psalm 137:4) We struggle not to lose our distinctiveness in that kind of environment.

Adlai Stephenson said, 'A free society is a society where it is safe to be unpopular.' On that definition, many workplaces are not free, so living our authenticity at work needs care. We must learn to resist the temptations either to suppress and marginalize our identity, or to present ourselves in a blunt and offensive way that alienates those around us. A natural response to a hostile culture can be either awkward and cowardly, or angry and confrontational. Neither response helps us or our colleagues. God's grace in us and through us is the supernatural response. We need a sensitive, diplomatic and authentic presence.

Back in the 1980s (before much of today's law on discrimination existed) I interviewed a man for a job and it became clear that he was a good candidate. Towards the end of the interview, he told me he was an orthodox Jew and explained that he had to be back in his north London Jewish community by sundown on Fridays to observe the Sabbath. To achieve this in winter, he would have to leave work shortly after lunch to have enough time for the commute. Although he was clearly nervous about telling me this, he promised that he would make up the time and asked if it would be possible. The guy was for real and I agreed. He was so grateful – and I cannot remember anyone I ever employed who worked as hard as he did. When he left on Fridays, nobody else in the team batted an eyelid. They wished him well.

Some years ago, I had to attend regular work meetings in San Francisco as part of a worldwide team. These meetings would begin on a Monday morning at 8.30 a.m. As I came from London, it was impossible for me to attend unless I left on Sunday morning. I mentioned to my American boss that, being a Christian, I normally attended church regularly with my family on a Sunday and asked if he would move the start time of a future meeting to a Tuesday morning. He did not agree at the time, but when the next meeting agenda arrived, it started on Tuesday morning. If only all my examples of sharing my Christian identity had such a positive outcome. Once I was asked at a business dinner to explain what my fish badge meant. After I had done so there was a long silence, followed by the lady opposite asking me, 'Are you a fanatic?'

It is possible to live by a different set of values in an alien environment without completely alienating everyone around you. It may be difficult, but it is not impossible. This is the challenge facing Christians in the workplace today: to retain an authentic, open Christian identity in a way that is diplomatic, tactful and able to engage with the culture around them. The challenge is both authenticity *and* credibility. Our authenticity will have a polarizing effect on people, just as Jesus did. On the one hand, most people appreciate others being real; on the other hand, no-one can please everyone. We will be tested. That test may be uncomfortable, or even painful.

When Satan challenged Jesus in the wilderness, the opening words of his temptation were, 'If you are the Son of God . . . ' (Matthew 4:3) The very first thing used to tempt Jesus was a challenge to his identity. In the nineteenth century people used to bite coinage to test whether it was authentic. The same thing is happening today with our identity. People want to put us under pressure to find out whether we are real, or whether we are like a *Star Trek* hologram – unreal. Sarcasm is a very common ploy, especially in a male environment. One of the most powerful ways for Christians to respond to difficult people in the workplace is to return insult with grace. Those who maintain their cool and their openness stand out in that kind of situation.

> A man's wisdom gives him patience;
> > it is to his glory to overlook an offence.
> (Proverbs 19:11)

There is something different about that, something interesting.

God's agenda in allowing our identity to be tested is different from the world's agenda. While others want to know if they can trust us, God is asking, 'Can you trust me?'

> To fear anyone will prove to be a snare,
> > but whoever trusts in the Lord is kept safe.
> (Proverbs 29:25 NIVI)

I find a helpful distinction between temptations and tests is that temptations are designed to make us fail, but tests are designed so we can succeed. As others put us under pressure to find our weaknesses and make us fail, God is allowing the pressure to refine us.

Insight Capture Questions
1. Where is my Christian identity under pressure?
2. What is my typical response to this pressure?

9. IN THE FURNACE

When you walk through the fire,
    you will not be burned;
the flames will not set you ablaze.
(Isaiah 43:2)

The symbol of fire in Scripture is often associated with God testing and refining the integrity of his people. Fire is a test of authenticity. Shadrach, Meshach and Abednego faced the fire of the furnace because they would not bow down to the statue of Nebuchadnezzar (Daniel 3). It was around the fire in the courtyard that Peter was challenged by the servant girl when she said he was 'one of them' (Mark 14:69). Often it is in the fiery cut and thrust of work and life that our true allegiance and identity are uncovered.

One of the best role models in Scripture for a believer in a hostile environment is Daniel, who was captured and then exiled to Babylon. He must have had every reason to feel a grievance against his captors, but none is described in the account of his life. Whatever hurt he may have taken at finding himself in a foreign culture with very limited freedom he seems to have forgiven. The example of Daniel is a testimony of grace under pressure – a powerful lesson in itself. He was free from past bitterness in order to be good news in the present. The supreme example, of course, is Jesus. When he was doing his greatest work, in appalling pain on the cross, the first thing he said was, 'Father, forgive them . . . ' (Luke 23:34) Is this something you need to do in your workplace?

Whether or not we feel like captives and exiles, we are unlikely to be good news if we are holding on to anger, bitterness or resentment. Feelings of being treated or paid unfairly, frustration with restrictions, inadequate systems and even verbal abuse can make the workplace a very angry and negative place. Forgiveness is not easy, but it is key to our mental and emotional health and important to maintaining our freedom to contribute positively to those around us.

Daniel must have been a very thoughtful man, who considered in advance the issues he was likely to face. He made some interesting choices that showed he would only confront the culture when his personal boundaries were at stake. Most importantly, he asked God for help and prayed to God regularly. This is a key principle on which he would not compromise even when an edict was issued against the practice (Daniel 6:10). He also resolved not to defile himself with the king's food, though he managed to negotiate this with quiet care and diplomatic tact. We must follow the same approach and decide carefully where we will draw the line in our environment. It is helpful and wise for us to anticipate potential issues that may arise in our situations and spend time thinking them through and praying about them in advance. The orthodox Jew I described in the previous chapter, who negotiated the ability to leave early on a Friday afternoon to celebrate the Sabbath, is a good example of someone with a clear boundary.

Daniel became an insider in the Babylonian culture and actively engaged with it by learning the language and customs. He accepted the different name his captors gave him because it did not define him – except to them. His courage, grace and forgiveness enabled him to mix with others who were very different, something that was no doubt rather uncomfortable on occasions. Through his diligence and excellent qualities he even rose to become an official with significant influence.

I have a feeling that the fruit of the Spirit was so evident in Daniel's life that when he did take a stand on an issue, his character had already won the battle. His obedient involvement in Babylonian society with his transparent Yahweh identity was done in a quiet yet confident way. Neil Anderson says, 'Humility is confidence properly placed in God, not ourselves.' Daniel was confident in God, and that was what gave him the calm ability to live and work as an authentic believer in an ungodly environment.

Being open about who we are is not the same thing as being naïve. Daniel never compromised his true identity, but neither was he 'in your face' about it. He adopted a non-confrontational, conciliatory attitude, exercising diplomacy and tact. Refusing a ghetto mentality in exile, he was ready to engage with the alien culture without being absorbed by it with the loss of his distinctiveness. He kept his commitment to God and won the respect even of King Nebuchadnezzar, the original 'boss from hell'.

Honesty pays

Sunita knew she hadn't made the cut last month and was trailing the others. She had spent too much time on low-value deals and checking up on clients to make sure everything had gone OK. Group bonus would be on the boss's radar. His culture was money, which is why he ran the agency. Sure enough, a text appeared on her mobile at 3 p.m. 'Ned wants to see you asap.' This could not be good.

Sunita felt fear and trepidation as she drove back to the office. She was certain this was it, the final nail in the coffin of her rejection. Parked outside, she breathed a request for God's grace to respond well to whatever Ned was going to say.

Fortunately, most of the others were out and the place was fairly quiet. Ned swivelled his chair round as Sunita knocked at the open door of the lion's den. 'Hi Sunita, have a seat. Do you know a man called Malcolm Goldsmith?' Sunita shook her head. Something in Ned's manner told her this was not disciplinary and her tension lessened slightly. 'He's an HR Manager for an American subsidiary, who need to find homes for some executives on a foreign assignment – and he wants you to handle it.' Her open mouth showed astonishment. 'Asked for you by name,' Ned continued, looking amused. 'He knows another client of yours – some girl called Amanda you placed last week. Apparently she told Malcolm you were totally trustworthy. These foreign executives are a gravy train for us – they always look for a nice place. If this guy trusts you, we're on to a winner. Looks like the rest of us will be thanking you for the bonus this month. Nice job!'

Sunita had a tough time, but eventually won respect. It does not always happen like this, but God has a habit of showing up when we least expect it. Even if the work scorecard is not always good, God's character can still shine through. 'But thanks be to God, who always leads us in triumphal procession in Christ and through us spreads everywhere the fragrance of the knowledge of him' (2 Corinthians 2:14). Sunita did not push her faith on to others. It was revealed through her character and her choice not to compromise on the truth.

Every Christian receives a new identity in Christ and every Christian at work will have that identity tested, proved and forged in the fire of the workplace. As our involvement with the world intensifies, so our engagement with God must also intensify. When we inevitably fail or compromise, God will use that failure to teach and refine us, as he did with King David. So a choice faces us. The choice is whether to make our relationship with God a priority. If we do not, other relationships will begin to define us and then our authenticity will be compromised. Identity is something we receive and also something we choose to become.

Insight Capture Questions
1. What issues might I face that could test my integrity?
2. Where am I avoiding involvement with the culture around me?

PART 2

MAKING THE RIGHT CHOICES

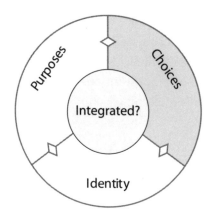

Figure 4

Accountability

Money

Time

Job change

Guidance

PART 2

MAKING THE RIGHT CHOICES

10. THE NAKED TRUTH?

Carry each other's burdens, and in this way you will fulfil the law of Christ.
(Galatians 6:2)

Old habits die hard

'I'm sick of it!' fumed Liz. 'No matter what you say, you're always late.'

'I'm not *always* late,' said Jack.

'Yes, you are,' she countered, 'and I'm absolutely fed up with it. You never get home for our evening meal on time. You call me from work and say you're going to be a little bit late. So I delay the meal, and then you turn up half an hour after that and the whole thing is ruined and I'm starving.'

Jack was on the defensive. 'I can't help it, it's the traffic.'

'That's not good enough,' retorted Liz. 'Traffic may be an issue sometimes, but not *every* night. Anyway, you could always call me from the car.'

'But I'm usually doing voicemail in the car.'

'Well, interrupt your wretched voicemail!' yelled Liz. There was a tense silence. 'Please, Jack, something's got to change here. I can't live like this, never being sure if you'll be home when you say.'

'Sorry,' said Jack.

'That's not good enough,' said Liz immediately. 'I accept that you're sorry and I forgive you; but you've got to find a way of fixing it.'

'What do you suggest?' asked Jack.

'I don't know. It's not my problem, it's your problem.'

'Thanks very much,' said Jack.

'You're welcome,' she replied. 'Now figure out a way of fixing it before I brain you. I'm going out for a walk.'

Jack heard the front door bang. 'Glad you remembered how to shut it,' he muttered.

Liz walked over to the park. The light was fading and there was no-one else around. 'God,' she shouted, 'please help Jack sort this out before I go mad. Please help him, Father, I don't know what else to do.' She paused. 'I'm sorry I shouted at Jack.'

She wandered on for another five minutes and then walked back home. Jack was sitting in the lounge, just staring into space when she came in. 'I'm sorry I shouted at you,' she said.

'It's OK,' said Jack, 'I probably deserved it. I'm sorry I keep being late.'

Liz sighed. 'I don't think I do deserve that.'

'I know,' said Jack.

The following Sunday, Jack was chatting with Mike after church and Jack thought he would ask his advice. 'Mind if I ask you something personal?' said Jack.

'Go ahead,' said Mike.

'Well, the thing is, I keep being late back from work and I think I may need somebody to help me change how I manage my time, give me a bit of coaching and pray for me.' They sat down on a couple of chairs. 'The thing is . . . well, I'll have to explain a bit more about what's going on at work and my life generally.'

They decided to get together for breakfast on Tuesday. 'Day after tomorrow it is,' said Mike, '7 a.m. at your place. Half an hour for breakfast, chat and pray. Great.'

On Tuesday Mike showed up bang on 7 a.m. Jack had his trousers on, but no shirt, when he opened the door. Mike laughed. 'I see the problem,' he said. 'I should have said 7.05.'

'No,' said Jack, 'I would still have been late.' They sat down to breakfast and gave thanks.

'The thing is,' said Jack, 'during the working day stuff happens that seems to expand what I have to get done before I come home. I try not to take anything back with me and I try to wrap up on all my voicemail when I'm coming home in the car.'

'Perfect for driving safely,' laughed Mike. Jack looked pained. 'Sorry,' said Mike.

'Anyway,' Jack continued, 'I know I should be going home, but I also know I can't leave with stuff undone, so I finish the work and then I'm late.'

He went on for five minutes with Mike clarifying things every so often. Eventually, Mike offered to pray and they both prayed. Then their conversation ranged over principles of time management, setting boundaries, dealing with difficult people and a host of other issues, until it was time to get to work. 'Better stop now,' said Mike. 'I don't want to make you late!'

Jack was grateful and felt encouraged. 'Thanks a lot, I really appreciate it.'

'No problem,' said Mike. 'What say we meet up in a week's time – next Tuesday still OK?'

The following Sunday, Mike asked Jack how it was going. 'Not great,' said Jack. 'A bit better. I was almost on time on Thursday and Liz nearly fainted.'

'Good,' said Mike.

'What, that she nearly fainted?'

'No, I mean well done that you managed to change something. What was it?'

'Well, I just decided I was going to let the monkey die.'

'Pardon?'

'We have this expression at work. When a task is delegated to you it's like a monkey clinging to your back. It's your monkey until you do it or delegate it to someone else. Well, I decided on Thursday that the monkey could stay clinging to my back and I would ignore it and see if it died.'

Mike laughed. 'Great! Did it die?'

'No. It bit me hard the following morning!' said Jack. 'Anyway, it was worth it for the expression on Liz's face.'

After a few weeks Jack was starting to make some progress and his friendship with Mike had deepened. One Tuesday morning Jack was ready at 7 a.m. on the dot, but Mike was late. He turned up at 7.10. 'You've done me a favour,' said Jack when Mike finished apologizing. 'Now I know how Liz feels.'

They sat down to breakfast and prayed. Strangely, Mike seemed a bit quiet afterwards. 'How's your work going?' asked Jack.

'OK,' said Mike, but his body language said something else.

After a pause, during which Mike looked at the table, Jack ventured, 'Something bothering you?'

There was another slight pause. 'Well, there is actually,' said Mike. 'To be honest, I haven't told anybody else.' He paused again and Jack waited patiently with a growing sense of unease. Mike looked out of the window for a moment. 'You know I work in Information Technology, so I get to visit a number of companies to implement computer systems. Well, recently I was at a company where I found someone was accessing pornography through their intranet. I reported it and the problem was fixed. They're no longer working there.' Mike sighed. 'At home that evening, Madge was out and I went back to the web-sites this guy had accessed and looked at them myself.'

Jack's brow furrowed. 'Why?'

'Curious, I suppose. I was tired and felt drawn to it. There are lots of links in that kind of stuff and, well . . . now I think I'm getting a bad habit.'

Jack tried not to show his shock. He felt out of his depth. Mike had just confessed he was becoming hooked on porn. Jack wasn't sure how to deal with this. 'You're happily married?' he quizzed.

'Yep, there's absolutely no reason why I should be doing this. In fact, I've noticed that since I have, my relationship with Madge has cooled.'

'Does she know about it?' Mike shook his head. 'Shouldn't you say something to Pastor Bob?'

'Yes,' said Mike, 'I will, but the prospect of talking to Bob is a bit intimidating and I'd like to be able to tell him I'm on the road to recovery. I know this needs to get sorted. I'd appreciate it if you'd pray for me, Jack. I know I can trust you.'

Jack prayed for Mike and the relief and thankfulness were evident in his eyes as the two of them parted company.

Next week they were both on time. 'How goes it?' asked Mike.

'Not great,' replied Jack. 'Failed four nights out of five and Liz is hopping mad. How about you?'

'Better. I lapsed once on Friday, but the rest of the week I was fine.'

The following day, Jack sent Mike a text at around 4 p.m. 'Three monkeys on my back – appreciate prayer.' Mike was sitting in front of his computer screen in the middle of something and, to be honest, could have done without it. However, he got up, walked over to the coffee machine via the loo and prayed for Jack. He prayed that God would somehow get those monkeys off Jack's back and give him the courage to keep to the boundaries he had set.

When he got back to his desk he replied, 'Praying 4u.'

That evening another text came. 'Thanks mate. Home on time. Liz over moon.'

Later that evening it was Jack's turn to get a text. His phone bleeped at around 9.30 p.m. Mike wrote, 'Appreciate your support now. Madge is out late.'

Jack sent a message back. 'For the eyes of the Lord range throughout the earth to strengthen those whose hearts are fully committed to him. 2 Chronicles 16:9. God bless.'

The London Institute for Contemporary Christianity did a survey in which they asked a sample of Christians in the UK what their needs were for better whole-life discipleship. Top of the list was a prayer partner. Christians in our society need and want somebody with whom they can pray and share the burdens of life. In our individualistic culture, we seem to have lost the pattern of behaviour that Jesus built into his disciples. He sent them out two by two (Luke 10:1).

Sometimes getting a request for immediate prayer can be inconvenient. Still, the fact is that both Jack and Mike improved in their behaviour and their practical holiness as a result of sharing and prayer.

For leaders especially, voluntary accountability is a critical discipline that is missing in too many situations. Every so often the press report on a leader who has 'crashed and burned' on some issue of sexual immorality, financial impropriety, or failure of some other kind. Most of the time the people concerned knew there was an issue and thought they could sort it out themselves. Now they are thinking, 'If only I'd had the support of somebody else.' Partnerships like that of Paul and Barnabas (Acts 11:26) and mentoring relationships like that of Paul and Timothy (Philippians 1:1) are a positive and important tool in whole-life discipleship and in strengthening the lives of believers.

Personal issues where we need support may be anything from a serious moral dilemma to a bad habit like lateness. Difficulties at work or family stress are other examples. Water in a barrel flows out through the lowest slat. We all have low slats in our barrel where life flows out. These may be areas where we are in a repetitive cycle of sin-confess, sin-confess, or situations where we simply need the opportunity to share and to be supported and encouraged.

Insight Capture Questions
1. What issues in my life would benefit from prayer support from another Christian?
2. Who might I ask to pray for me?

11. WHO CAN I TRUST?

A friend loves at all times,
  and a brother is born for adversity.
(Proverbs 17:17)

Ouch

Liz was so pleased about Jack's improvement. When he was occasionally late it was less of an issue, because she knew he had listened to her, taken her seriously and was making an effort. They were chatting one evening and she said, 'Jack, I just want to say again how grateful I am that you're coming home on time.'

'Well, it was meeting with Mike. His support and prayer has made a real difference. In fact, I think it's made a difference to him too.'

'Really?'

'Yeah, there were a few issues he was having with some guys at work accessing pornography and he felt a bit drawn into it.' As soon as the words were out of his mouth, Jack knew he had done the wrong thing. 'Um, sorry, you shouldn't know about that.'

'Yes, I wish you hadn't told me,' sighed Liz. 'Now you've burdened me with private information about the husband of one of my friends and I'm going to feel really awkward.'

Jack clenched his jaw. 'I need to be more careful,' he said to himself quietly.

Liz nodded. 'I don't want to know anything else

that you two talk about. I'm just glad you're getting together to pray.'

Jack felt uncomfortable when Mike turned up the following Tuesday, but he started upbeat. 'Mike, I've made it back on time four times this week and I'm starting to get into the habit. The thing I found hardest, but really effective, was building in some margin in my diary around 4 p.m. Blindingly obvious when you think about it, but I just had so many back-to-back things going on in the day that I had no spare time.'

'Great,' said Mike.

They munched on cereal for a minute or two. Jack shifted uneasily on his chair. 'Mike, I've got another problem.'

'Don't tell me,' said Mike, 'you're early!'

'No, it's not about timing,' said Jack. 'Mike, I'm really sorry, but when Liz was telling me how great it was to have me home on time, I told her about our meetings and I let slip about the porn.' Mike coloured up and Jack could see that he was really angry. 'I didn't mean to tell her,' he said, 'and I am really sorry, Mike.'

'Has she told Madge?'

'No, definitely not. I checked and she won't either. In fact, Liz was really cross with me about having let it slip.'

Mike stared at the table and was silent for a while. 'I can't pretend I'm not disappointed, Jack,' he said. 'I thought I could trust you.'

'You can trust me,' said Jack. 'If you couldn't trust me, I wouldn't have told you.'

Mike nodded. 'Yeah, you're right.'

After a moment's reflection, Mike said, 'You know, this is my fault.'

'Why?' asked Jack.

'Well, if, when we started, we had set the expectations for our prayer and support together, we could have had some understanding that would have prevented this. Confidentiality would have been part of it. I can hardly complain, because I told Madge about your lateness problem.'

Trust is absolutely essential to an effective relationship. Nobody is perfect and we will be disappointed if we expect our Christian friends to be perfect, but we must be able to trust each other. Trust requires confidentiality, dignity, reliability and the willingness to be open and honest in a gracious way.

> Discretion will protect you,
>> and understanding will guard you.
> (Proverbs 2:11)

(There are some legitimate limits to confidentiality. In rare scenarios, something may be shared where the listener may be legally obligated to report it. For example, if they suspect that a child or an elderly person is currently endangered by abuse, or if the person is a danger to themselves or others. These are highly unusual situations, however.)

Secondly, a voluntary accountability partner or group is not a substitute for God. Ownership of my issues belongs with me, not others. I am primarily accountable to God for my own work and life. 'So then, we will all give an account of ourselves to God' (Romans 14:12 NIVI). There are two ways in which accountability partners can fall into a trap in this area. The first is if a co-dependency develops which is unhealthy. If your prayer partner is calling you too frequently to plead for your support, they may be unwittingly putting you in the position of God. The second is if you are too assertive or proactive in repeatedly checking up on them. Then you are putting yourself in a position of ownership and responsibility that does not belong to you. Some churches have had problems like this where people have been not only accountable, but oppressed by others who have fallen into the trap of playing God.

Godly advice is often better given through a thoughtful question rather than an attempt at direction. One example of a question that encourages someone to take ownership could be, 'If you were advising someone else in your situation, what would you recommend?'

In the same way that prayer partners are not a substitute for God, neither are they a substitute for the church or for the advice of church leaders where appropriate. A prayer partner's role is to be an encourager, who can help another person engage with God. If a problem is shared, it is primarily for the purpose of prayer. It can be helpful to remind each other of scriptures that are relevant, but the primary responsibility is to pray and encourage your partner to pray. We must never be deceived about where our help comes from. 'My help comes from the LORD' (Psalm 121:2). Whether the need is to break a habit, determine the right course of action, or overcome depression, ultimately God is the one who meets our need.

> The LORD sets prisoners free,
>   the LORD gives sight to the blind,
> the LORD lifts up those who are bowed down.
> (Psalm 146:7–8)

Finally, prayer partners should be of the same sex, to avoid the obvious problem of inappropriate intimacy. Although married couples can act as accountability partners for each other to a degree, there are limits to how well this works because of the emotional involvement. Generally, I think it is better to find someone else.

After meeting to pray with a friend, it is often a good idea to spend a few moments praying on our own. This gives us the opportunity to turn over to God whatever was shared, asking God to refresh and cleanse our mind from anything negative or tempting and helping us to forget unhelpful details.

Voluntary accountability is an act of faith. It is trusting God enough to believe he can work through other people in our lives. Jesus shared his deepest feelings with his closest friends and sought their support (Matthew 26:38). So can we.

Each of us work and live in the context of a network of key relationships (see figure 5). I find it helpful to picture this

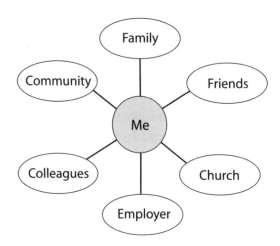

Figure 5

as being like one atom linked to other atoms inside a personal molecule. These key relationships are the stakeholders in my life – my family, my friends, my church, my employer, my work colleagues and my community. One way to extend the benefit of voluntary accountability is to seek feedback from these people.

On the next page is a short questionnaire that can prompt a useful dialogue between some of our stakeholders and ourselves. It takes courage to ask for feedback, because we guess it might not be what we want to hear. Yet seeking this kind of input can help us to hear God's voice through others.

Sometimes we can easily be preoccupied with activity or success in statistical or financial terms, but excellence in Scripture is defined more in terms of relationships and character (1 Corinthians 13:1; Psalm 45:2). A life open to the input of other people is a life more likely to be healthy and balanced.

Occasionally, I have found it helpful to ask a few people to meet as a reference group for a specific situation or project. Others whom I trust and who take an interest can pray for me and give me a 'sanity check'. My experience is that when my friends understand more of my situation, I have been amazed by their encouragement, creativity and support.

Stakeholder Questionnaire

A questionnaire for your friends and family about your work-life integration.

LICC prepared this list of questions with Christian singles, married people and families in mind. All the same, we recognize that married people and families have particular issues not always faced by singles, so there are a few extra questions for these people at the end.

How to use it: give it to your partner, family member or friend, and let them answer the questions as though you are asking them. We recommend that they write down their answers to the questions and then discuss the answers with you.

1. Do you think that I have got stuck in habits that detract from my ability to integrate work and non-work aspects of my life? What are those habits?

2. On a scale of 1 to 5, rate how 'with' you I am when we're together. Do I occasionally, often or always seem distracted and 'elsewhere'?

3. From the way that I talk about my work, do you sense that it's an area of my life in which Christ and my faith have a definite and distinctive impact?

4. Do you think I have the right attitude to work and relaxation?

5. What role could you play in helping me achieve a better standard of work-life integration?

6. Do you believe I am sufficiently accountable to you for the choices and priorities in my work and life?

7. Do you believe that I am living a life with clear purpose?

8. As far as you are able to discern, how consistent are my work and life with God's calling for me?

Additional questions for spouses and families

9. As far as you are able to discern, how consistent are my work and life with God's calling for us as a family?

10. On a scale of 1 to 5, how would you rate the ability of our family to manage the pressures of work and life? Do we need to make any changes?

12. BREAKING THE POWER OF MONEY

Where your treasure is, there your heart will be also.
(Matthew 6:21)

Onwards and upwards

He knew it was a bit irregular, but it wouldn't do any harm. He could increase the quarter-end stats by accelerating some large shipments. That would result in a nice little pay bonus – just enough to solve his immediate need. Next quarter it would all even out. If customers returned goods he could hide the reversal by using some accounting code until business caught up again.

Gordon was happy to be back. It had been ten years since he emigrated to the States. Now he had a one-year foreign assignment as interim General Manager back on his old home turf. The local HR Manager had fixed him up with a great housing agent and they had found a place near Ascot. It was a bit more than the company's allowance, but he figured it was worth it if it kept Cheryl happy.

Hers was a 'rags to riches' story. Brought up in an east London council flat, she had met the young executive Gordon at a club. He enjoyed wowing her with his wealth, but over the years her aspirations had grown. She had become accustomed to a materially driven lifestyle and Gordon had become sucked into making more and more money. Cheryl's latest demand was for a little holiday pad in Cyprus. That was what was stretching Gordon's resources and making him think more creatively about how to increase his already substantial pay.

Financial pressure never goes away, does it? Money is always bidding for our attention, always bidding for control of our lives. It is either the pressure of not enough money, or the responsibility of deciding what to do with our wealth. When Jesus said, 'You cannot serve both God and Money' (Matthew 6:24), he did not disqualify us from having wealth. He meant that we cannot follow the real God if we have allowed money to gain power over us. Those whose lives are controlled by wealth are in just as much bondage as those who are in debt.

People like Cheryl, who have had little money, cannot imagine that too much has an evil side. The power to buy is heady stuff. Money is not just a thing, it has a power and that power can be hazardous to our spiritual health. It has the potential of becoming a god that competes for our devotion. We can easily be tempted to become selfish, self-satisfied, materialistic, arrogant and totally indifferent to others. Money can give people a false sense of security. Things become mine – my toys, my money and my property. Affluent people sometimes find themselves enjoying the quiet superiority of having more money than their less fortunate friends. They never imagine that they themselves are being sucked in by a spiritual power seeking to enslave them.

Since work is a means to deliver more money, the seductive power of wealth can easily translate into pursuing choices at work that are unwise. Money may make us take the wrong job or drive us to try to get promoted too early.

The deception that more money is always good can cause stress, loss of job satisfaction and a working lifestyle that threatens relationships. All in the name of owning and controlling more wealth.

A few years ago, my dad was given control of the finances of an older relative who became mentally incapable. It was done under a power of attorney, which granted him the legal right to control all the other person's money and affairs until death. In a situation like that, when it is somebody else's money, handling it feels different. It is different. It was a big responsibility and I was impressed by the care and diligence of my dad.

The Bible says that all our money and all our possessions belong to someone else. We own nothing, and everything we earn and spend and save and give is somebody else's money. ' "The silver is mine and the gold is mine," declares the LORD Almighty' (Haggai 2:8). 'The earth is the LORD's, and everything in it' (Psalm 24:1). It is all God's money. We do not ultimately own anything. We have been given free will to decide what to do with it, but our so-called legal ownership is really just a tool for us to handle what belongs to God. How does that make you feel?

A rich person was once asked how much was enough, to which he replied, 'Just a little more.' Owning wealth does not necessarily bring contentment and peace and for some people, contentment can never be attained however much they have. In fact, contentment starts with the realization that nothing really belongs to us. That truth frees us from a lot of problems. Once we have grasped it, our whole world-view changes.

One important, practical way to break the power of wealth is to give it away. Generosity motivated by love breaks the hold of money and confuses selfish people.

When Mary broke the alabaster jar of perfume over Jesus, she was immediately criticized by Judas, who said, 'Why this waste?' But Jesus said, 'She has done a beautiful thing to me' (Mark 14:4–6; John 12:4–5). Giving is a beautiful thing because it imitates the character of God.

We can give cheerfully because it is not our money anyway! Giving is a trusting and joyful response to God's love and grace. Giving a tenth (tithing) is the only time in Scripture when God invites us to test him.

> 'Bring the whole tithe into the storehouse, that there may be food in my house. Test me in this,' says the LORD Almighty, 'and see if I will not throw open the floodgates of heaven and pour out so much blessing that you will not have room enough for it.'
> (Malachi 3:10)

There are some situations where tithing may not be appropriate – for example, if it means delaying the settlement of a personal debt, or depriving another family member of much-needed care (Mark 7:11). In other situations, tithing may be an inadequate response to the wealth God has put in our care. Scripture teaches generally that our giving should be proportional to our means (1 Corinthians 16:1–2; 2 Corinthians 8:1–15). Many Christians use 10% as a starting point for their giving. Far from being a legalistic command, tithing is an opportunity to honour God – and God honours those who honour him (1 Samuel 2:30). We may not get back God's blessing in cash, but the experience of countless Christians is that God does bless those who give, and he meets our needs.

Giving is also a *future-oriented* activity of faith. The Bible likens giving to sowing seed. It changes the future for both the recipient and the giver – and in time it will produce a harvest. Exercising our faith and doing our giving while we are living can produce remarkable results. We can also make an important and positive difference to future generations through our wills when we have to give everything away. 'Good people leave an inheritance for their children's children' (Proverbs 13:22 NIVI).

Another important way to break the power of wealth in our lives is to practise the spiritual discipline of simplicity – choosing to use money for needs, not for wants. Peer pressure at work to wear the 'right' clothes or drive the 'right' car can influence us to spend money on our image to satisfy the need for acceptance, or on status symbols to satisfy the need to feel significant. Our 'impulse buys' are often driven by emotional needs. Simplicity means resisting those underlying psychological drives to satisfy our cravings or pander to our insecurities. 'Those who would come after me must deny themselves and take up their cross and follow me' (Matthew 16:24 NIVI).

Choosing a simple lifestyle is not living in deprivation or poverty, it is the quiet and thoughtful decision to focus resources on what matters. Not many people bother to stop and think about what really matters, but doing so can have unexpected spin-off benefits. A simple lifestyle reduces the 'noise' of life's distractions and gives greater inner peace and contentment. It improves our ability to enjoy things. People who have chosen a simple lifestyle are better equipped to deal with the impact of a sudden change like losing a job.

This does not mean that poor Christians are better than rich Christians, because all Christians have the same status before God as adopted children (John 1:12). Actually I know a few rich Christians who practise simplicity and are also very generous. Many of them I consider to be exceptional disciples. God has appointed us all 'power of attorney' over some of his affairs. It is not the amount of money that matters; it is what we choose to do with it.

Setting a budget and buying things more carefully and cheaply frees up money, which can then be used for a better purpose – doing good to others. Some of Jesus' teaching requires us to do things that cannot be done without money, like providing for our family and giving to the poor. No-one would have remembered the Good Samaritan if he had only good intentions. He also had money that he had saved, and he used it well (Luke 10:35). John Wesley said, 'Earn all you can, save all you can, give all you can.'

Amongst our work colleagues the talk may be about what we own, but Jesus asks, 'What have you done with what I own and have entrusted to your care?' Prosperity is an instrument to be used, not a deity to be worshipped. What are we doing to use wealth in a way that honours God and blesses others?

Insight Capture Questions
1. If I lost my money and possessions, what would happen to my self-worth?
2. What proportion of my wealth do I give away?
3. How might I live more simply?
4. What provision have I made for the future? Have I made a will?

13. BEYOND MY MEANS?

Let no debt remain outstanding, except the continuing debt to love one another.
(Romans 13:8)

Oh no

Jane felt a familiar sick feeling in the pit of her stomach as she looked at the letter. Since her husband had left her, it had been impossible to live only on her pay. At breakfast she had put off opening the statement. Last month she hadn't known how to deal with the rising debt and had just let the interest accumulate. She had lost track of exactly how much she owed and knew she was about to find out.

After putting the children to bed, Jane steeled herself to open the letter and as she read it she let out a gasp. 'Oh God, what am I going to do?' She sat with her head in her hands and an overwhelming fear seemed to wash over her. She felt like running away. Way over her credit limit, she faced a demand for repayment. If she made this payment, there wouldn't be enough for the rent and she was already late with that.

Debt had been her only lifeline. Now that was being taken away from her, she was desperate. She wanted to make something happen, but had no idea what to do. Jane felt completely alone. 'How can I possibly survive?' she thought. 'If I get a second job, I'll have to pay for more childcare. Then I'll hardly get to see my own children.' She burst into tears.

Recent figures show that consumer and mortgage debt in the Western world is rocketing. In an economy where the high cost of housing means it is sometimes difficult to live close to where you work, options are limited and the temptation to borrow too much can be hard to resist. Credit and loan adverts are in our faces on television screens and the internet all the time. As I write, record levels of personal bankruptcy have just been reported. That shows how much of an issue debt is.

There are two routes into debt:

- when life's difficult circumstances mean that you cannot survive without borrowing;
- when you choose to borrow, because you want something you cannot afford.

People in debt experience a wide range of emotional problems. Mild anxiety can give way to depression and to a real degeneration in health. Marital or family breakdown and even child abuse and suicides have been traced to debt. Children do not know much about money. They do not respect the problem and a parent who is in debt is a stressed parent, trying not to feel a failure, trying to overcome the impossible. People in debt are at risk of being led astray. At the end of their tether, desperation tempts some people into crime.

> . . . give me neither poverty nor riches,
>   but give me only my daily bread . . .
> Or I may become poor and steal,
>   and so dishonour the name of my God.
> (Proverbs 30:8–9)

Is there hope for someone in debt? How can we recover from it and get back to a better financial position?

Hope – the story of the widow of Zarephath

The wife of a man from the company of the prophets cried out to Elisha, 'Your servant my husband is dead, and you know that he revered the LORD. But now his creditor is coming to take my two boys as his slaves.'

Elisha replied to her, 'How can I help you? Tell me, what do you have in your house?'

'Your servant has nothing there at all,' she said, 'except a little oil.'

Elisha said, 'Go round and ask all your neighbours for empty jars. Don't ask for just a few. Then go inside and shut the door behind you and your sons. Pour oil into all the jars, and as each is filled, put it to one side.'

She left him and afterwards shut the door behind her and her sons. They brought the jars to her and she kept pouring. When all the jars were full, she said to her son, 'Bring me another one.'

But he replied, 'There is not a jar left.' Then the oil stopped flowing.

She went and told the man of God, and he said, 'Go, sell the oil and pay your debts. You and your sons can live on what is left.'

(2 Kings 4:1–7)

This story has some useful principles in it. First and foremost, God is willing to help us with money problems when we turn to him. God is compassionate and the widow's appeal to the prophet Elisha resulted in a response that transformed the situation.

Secondly, it shows that we need the help of other people – not necessarily always in the form of money, but help in other ways too. It can be very hard admitting to financial difficulties, and it takes courage and humility to ask for help. Someone in debt has to learn to accept help from other people and overcome that initial feeling of failure.

Thirdly, God wants us to repay our debts – that is what the prophet commanded the widow to do. The Bible does not forbid or condemn debt, but does make repaying it a priority. 'Let no debt remain outstanding, except the continuing debt to love one another' (Romans 13:8). Repaying debts is important, because when we borrow money we sacrifice some freedom and until the debt is cleared, the past is still influencing our future. 'The borrower is servant to the lender' (Proverbs 22:7). Jesus does not want money to be the master of our lives. As anyone in debt can tell you, it feels like being locked up by the past. It puts us in survival mode and into a slavish routine that sometimes feels like trying to climb out of a deep pit.

Another lesson from the story is that we have to cooperate with God in order to work our way out of debt. The widow had to do some work – in this case getting jars from others, pouring oil into them and selling it. The flow of oil for her was a miracle, but the principle is that God is the one who enables us to produce wealth through our work (Deuteronomy 8:18).

Overall, the lesson I take from this passage is that there is hope and a way out of debt. It may not be easy, but the past does not have to totally control our future. God can bring freedom in place of captivity, thankfulness in place of despair, peace in place of anxiety.

In the Old Testament law God showed his concern about people trapped by debt. He gave a command to cancel all debts every seven years and return all land to its original owners every fifty years in what was termed a Jubilee year, when slaves were also released (Deuteronomy 15:1; Leviticus 25). This Jubilee principle effectively eliminated the risk of people being in permanent bondage. Israel never properly obeyed that law, but in the early church we read, 'Selling their possessions and goods, they gave to anyone who had need' (Acts 2:45 NIVI) – a fantastic picture of the principle being lived out. No needy people means nobody in crippling debt. The same should and could be true in our churches today.

If you are in debt and need help, then one place you can call in the UK is the Consumer Credit Helpline: 0800 1381111. Credit Action (on the internet at www.creditaction.org.uk) is another organization, run by Christians, that produces resources to help people manage their financial affairs.

Insight Capture Questions
1. How are my work-life decisions being influenced by debt?
2. Which of the lessons from the story of the widow of Zarephath might apply to me?

14. DRIVEN AND DECEIVED

What good is it for you to gain the whole world, yet forfeit your soul?
(Mark 8:36 NIVI)

Trapped?

It was dark as Fred rolled into the station car park in his BMW 5 series. After buying the *Financial Times*, he stood on the freezing platform waiting for the 6.03 a.m. train to London. If it was on time, the journey would take one hour and fifty-five minutes from his home in the country to his desk in Canary Wharf. It *was* on time! He found a window seat and looked at the front page. In five minutes he was asleep. Arriving at work, his first task was to empty a sachet of decongestant powder into a cup of boiling water from the coffee machine. Trying to ignore the cold he knew was gaining on him, he sat down with just enough time to clear his emails before the markets began in earnest.

It had been a difficult weekend. His wife became upset when he fell asleep after lunch on Saturday – she had wanted to go shopping. The kids had nagged on and on about what they wanted for Christmas. The ride-on mower had developed a fault. Church had just passed him by. The whole thing was a blur, just like the screen in front of him.

'Hi Fred, here we go again. Gluttons for punishment, but it pays the mortgage, eh?'

'Yeah, only seventeen years to go,' he replied.

Just past 8 p.m., Fred rolled back into the drive of his upmarket home. Around fourteen hours door to door. Ten hours left to read the mail, unwind, sleep, shower and drive back to the station. Oh, and spend some quality time with his family, half of whom were already asleep.

In today's economy, housing costs are often high and that can mean it is tough to make ends meet – especially when you buy your first house. But when people start to trade up every time they are promoted, they can get sucked into higher mortgages and financial commitments that lock them into a materially driven lifestyle. Money becomes more important than time. How many people in their thirties or forties only go home to sleep on weekdays, because the rest of their life is driven by the need to service their mortgage and consumer debt? The unspoken competition over the standard of housing and cars is literally killing some people with stress. Families are being wrecked with relational breakdown brought on by absence and no energy left after work.

In the context of integrating work and life, it is important to preserve freedom of choice. Yet many mortgage themselves into a situation where the debt undermines any ability to choose an alternative. 'Gearing up' can mean being afraid to change job, afraid of the financial challenge of Christmas and afraid to tell others about the reality of the mental pressure. Sometimes it is not only our houses that we mortgage, but our choices as well.

Using credit like this assumes a future that is uncertain. It is one thing to borrow money against an asset with sensible

repayments when we know we have the capability to repay.
Yet it is reckless to have such a high level of borrowing that
we cannot recover if any major change occurs – like redundancy, illness or a family crisis. Living a lower-debt lifestyle is
a bit like planning a margin into our day. We know we are
going to need it to help us deal with the unexpected.

In order to live a low-debt lifestyle, we first have to choose
to face up to the issue and ask ourselves what is really driving
our choices. That may not be as simple as it seems. On the
surface, there is something we need or want that does not
sound too unreasonable, but underneath there are psychological needs. The deceptive power of spending money is in
appearing to meet those needs. If that is what is happening,
then we are subtly transferring our worship of God to things.
Instead of trusting God to meet our needs, we start trusting
our idols to meet them.

Difficult choices may be necessary. It is one thing to
decide to do our shopping elsewhere to save money, or even
perhaps not to have a holiday this year. It is something else
to decide to downsize our house, or to sell our car, or alter
our choice of schooling or healthcare, or change our work
in order to reduce debt. Yet living a low-debt lifestyle is an
important principle, which becomes more and more necessary as we grow older. Income levels tend to fall in later life,
and if we have not become used to living in a low-debt way,
it can be a hard landing.

Many become long-term victims of their short-term
choices. We must be people who are not in bondage to anything. Experience shows that good advisers help a lot.

> Plans fail for lack of counsel,
>> but with many advisers they succeed.
> (Proverbs 15:22)

It might be helpful to have someone else to share with as we make financial choices and changes.

Whether debt has been forced on you or chosen by you, it is important to have a viable plan to eliminate it, preferably with the support of others. Learning to live a low-debt lifestyle is a key principle for successfully integrating work and life.

Down the pan

Gordon's pressure from Cheryl was rising. The money for a deposit on the Mediterranean villa had over-stretched him. Things he would never have considered doing were now becoming commonplace. What had started as accelerated deliveries had developed into a wider range of ploys to get money more quickly. Financing deals, project management services paid for up-front, bogus orders that were really just letters of intent – Gordon knew all the tricks of the trade. Unfortunately, so did the auditors, and their trail eventually caught up with Gordon. He was sum-moned back to the States for a very uncomfortable meeting.

The shock was numbing. Everything he had worked for was falling down around him. His self-worth based on money crashed with his job loss. Gordon did not know how he could face Cheryl and the family. Lucky to escape a legal action, the career and the life he had lived based on acquisition were over.

Those who want to get rich fall into temptation and a trap and into many foolish and harmful desires that plunge people into ruin and destruction. For the love

> of money is a root of all kinds of evil. Some people,
> eager for money, have wandered from the faith and
> pierced themselves with many griefs.
> (1 Timothy 6:9–10 NIVI)

Not all financially driven people are ethically compromised, but the temptation is there. In terms of spiritual health, we are possibly more at risk from wealth than we are from poverty.

> You say, 'I am rich; I have acquired wealth and do not need a thing.' But you do not realise that you are wretched, pitiful, poor, blind and naked.
> (Revelation 3:17)

As we seek to live as whole-life disciples, wealth can be a blind spot, subtly undermining our ability to make wise choices.

If your life is driven by money, then you have a rival god (Matthew 6:24), a root of evil (1 Timothy 6:9–11) and a deception (Revelation 3:16–17). Jesus said, ' . . . the worries of this life, the deceitfulness of wealth and the desires for other things come in and choke the word, making it unfruitful' (Mark 4:19). In contrast, if your heart is to honour God, then the power of money will be broken. It will become your servant and a blessing to you (Ecclesiastes 5:19), a blessing to others (Luke 6:38), and will be used for non-financial goals as a way of obtaining true spiritual riches (Luke 16:10–12). God wants us to master money, not be mastered by it. As Spurgeon said, 'Money is the servant of the wise but the master of fools.'

Managing wealth to the glory of God and the good of others is a great ministry. It is a tension between, on the one hand, the scripture that says 'Do not worry' (Matthew 6:25) and, on the other hand, the parable of the talents, which tells us to use carefully all that we have received (Matthew 25:14–30). It is faith combined with effort, and tranquillity without complacency. Good stewardship involves both self-denial and a deep satisfaction and contentment; it blesses our families, our community and the wider world.

Insight Capture Questions
1. How much does financial pressure drive my lifestyle?
2. What decisions could I take to achieve greater financial freedom?

15. GOT RHYTHM?

Walk with me and work with me – watch how I do it. Learn the unforced rhythms of grace.
(Matthew 11:29 *The Message*)

Same old stuff

Tom was fed up with his job. As a fitter, all he did was turn up, follow the design, build it and then move on to the next place. One of the better fitters, he liked carpentry and making things, but just felt like a cog in the company machine. His job lacked a sense of wholeness and Tom felt dissatisfied and frustrated. He wanted to be more involved with the planning and customer feedback – to see the job through to the end.

Though he was expected to produce quality work, Tom was measured on how long it took him. The faster he did it, the better his performance. Correction: the faster he did it, the better *their* performance. For some time now, Tom had been thinking seriously of going out on his own. The big worry was whether he would be able to find enough work. Theoretically he could make a lot more money, but money wasn't the main issue. He wanted the satisfaction of seeing the whole job through, from design to payment, with a happy customer at the end.

Sue had a similar problem. Working at a call centre, her job was to answer the telephone with a pre-set script. Every day was the same – repetitive and boring.

There was hardly any planning involved, little feed-back, and definitely no sense of satisfaction. Whenever something interesting came up, she had to escalate it to the supervisor.

Over 35 years of research by Professor Sir Michael Marmot of University College London Hospitals has led him to the conclusion that poor health amongst workers is caused as much by badly designed jobs as it is by smoking, lack of exercise and poor diet. Treating people like machines in the workplace appears to reduce life expectancy measurably. Disempowered jobs and dysfunctional teams are a health hazard.

The high rate of staff turnover in call centres and the boredom felt on factory production lines are partly because staff are only doing part of the whole job. Auditors can also end up feeling unsatisfied and often move on after a few years, because there is less long-term satisfaction in only checking other people's work. People want to do their own work. When Volvo introduced a new working pattern, with small groups of workers responsible for making the whole car, quality and satisfaction improved significantly.

Some years ago there was a programme on television called *Masterclass*. It showed accomplished musicians teaching younger, talented musicians how to play. I remember one scene where a master cellist was leaning over the student with his hand on the bow, guiding the playing. That image stayed with me as a picture of how God can have his hand on our working patterns. The Master Craftsman has ways of working which are revealed in Scripture.

Christian Schumacher, reflecting on the creation narrative in Genesis, has pointed out that one of God's ways is that first he plans, then he does, and finally he evaluates what he has done. Why did God not make the world in a single act? It would not have been a problem to him. Instead he planned the grand project of creation as a series of steps, culminating with humankind. In each of these steps, he had a vision and a completion. Huge tasks are much easier if they are broken down into small jobs. I am following this pattern of planning now as I write this book – breaking the book into chapters and then thinking through the different parts of each chapter.

Having planned it, God then did the work of creation. For each step of creation he said, 'Let there be . . . ' and there was (Genesis 1). Then we see his evaluation step: 'And God saw that it was good.' There is an important principle here for effective work: plan, do, review.

Perhaps the supreme example of this is the cross and resurrection. The cross was planned by God and known about in advance (Matthew 16:21). Jesus undertook his atoning work on the cross with complete commitment and as he died, he said, 'It is finished.' When God evaluated the work on the cross, he ripped the temple curtain in two and then raised Jesus from the dead – vindicating his work as well as confirming his identity.

When I was in management, I used to have back-to-back meetings throughout the working day. Then I changed my working pattern and introduced longer gaps between meetings. During these gaps I reviewed what had been done in the previous session and made sure actions were followed up. Then I planned for the next session. I tried to treat each one of these meetings as a separate item of work, which must be planned, done and reviewed. As a result I had fewer meetings, yet somehow became more effective! It was partly this different working pattern that enabled me to be sufficiently effective to move to a four-day working week, while holding a director-level position in a large company.

Creation contains various rhythms that are designed to govern our work patterns. The first pattern is night and day. 'As long as it is day, we must do the work of him who sent me. Night is coming, when no-one can work' (John 9:4). The second pattern is weekly rest. When man and woman were created on the sixth day, their first experience was rest on the seventh day. So we were created both to work from rest and rest from work. This is God's pattern. 'The seventh day is a Sabbath to the LORD your God. On it you shall not do any work . . . ' (Exodus 20:10) The third pattern is seasonal change, where work changes from ploughing to sowing to growing to harvesting. God has designed work to be done in rhythms of fruitfulness. He has also designed the workers with bodies that have healthy rhythms, like heartbeat and breathing and sleep.

If we try to ride roughshod over these creation patterns, we become stressed in our work, we lose effectiveness and we can lose our health. Modern-day examples of this abound in our workplaces. Many experience intense periods of activity when deadlines loom. If these deadlines involve large projects, the work can go on and on at a frantic pace, seven days a week, for months. People begin to lose their concentration and start to burn out. When the project is finished, there is total exhaustion and often extended absence. Businesses try to dignify this kind of experience with the term 'managed intensity', but the reality is that overwork followed by binge resting goes against the principles of God's rhythms of fruitfulness. 'Even during the ploughing season and harvest you must rest' (Exodus 34:21). Time off sick or exhausted becomes the Sabbaths in arrears.

Only people who know they are justified by the unearned grace of God can truly rest in God's rhythms without guilt.

As Tim Chester says, 'God does not expect me to do more than I can. Our obsession with efficiency and productivity is a reflection of an achievement-centred spirituality.' This is an ancient heresy – salvation or sanctification by works in another guise. 'Are you so foolish? After beginning with the Spirit, are you now trying to attain your goal by human effort?' (Galatians 3:3)

The agricultural model of growth is something worth thinking about. Trees cannot produce more fruit by trying harder or working more efficiently; they produce fruit when they are cared for properly. When a tree is pruned and has enough light, nutrients and water and is protected so that it does not suffer from viruses or pests, it produces good-quality fruit. The same principles apply to us. Although in the short term we can vary energy and output, in the long run it is whether we are cared for, nourished and kept healthy that determines whether we will be fruitful.

Jesus chose to work with others on earth. He also sent out the disciples two by two. For us to be effective in our work, we need to work in cooperation with other people. Not necessarily in formalized organizations, but in work groups that will accomplish more than an individual could achieve.

> Two are better than one,
>> because they have a good return for their work:
> If they fall down,
>> one can help the other up.
> But pity those who fall
>> and have no friend to help them up!

Also, if two lie down together, they will keep warm.
But how can one keep warm alone?
Though one may be overpowered,
two can defend themselves.
A cord of three strands is not quickly broken.
(Ecclesiastes 4:9–12 NIVI)

A friend of mine tells a story of a manufacturing expert who used to be called in from head office to fix difficult technical problems. He enjoyed high self-esteem based on his unique knowledge of the technology, but he was a loner. When the technology changed, he found himself completely sidelined, because he had no relationship with the rest of the organization. People who choose an isolated working approach eventually find themselves left out. In the long run, relational skills are important for employability and effectiveness.

God's pattern of working is open for all to see. The more we can adopt his patterns, the more fruitful we will be. Jesus said, 'Anyone who chooses to do the will of God will find out whether my teaching comes from God or whether I speak on my own' (John 7:17 NIVI). It worked for me.

Insight Capture Questions
1. Which part of Plan/Do/Review am I most inclined to miss out in my work?
2. What healthy rhythm is missing or distorted in my work/life?
3. Which of my working relationships needs most attention?

16. HIGH TIME

Be still, and know that I am God.
(Psalm 46:10)

All too much

Andrew frowned as he noticed the flickering petrol warning light. After a late start that morning he had forgotten to fill up. Work had been non-stop and he felt exhausted. Turning into a side road, he pulled over by a farm gate leading to a field and switched off the ignition. He rubbed his eyes as the engine cooled down with a series of contracting clicks and then gazed for a while at the animals grazing in the field. A bird hopped onto a branch in the hedge and stared at him. Gratefully he let the silence envelop him, closed his eyes and felt the tiredness like a blanket. Andrew prayed for strength for the rest of the day and for what lay ahead in the weeks and months to come.

The three months leading up to Christmas had been the most stressful he had ever experienced. Work had been exceptionally busy, with several foreign trips, and he had found it impossible to organize a time when everyone could rehearse a sketch for the Christmas service. At home his teenage daughter was becoming tetchy – preparing for mock examinations due right after the holiday. Linda was trying to keep the household together with all the pre-Christmas activity. Perhaps most worrying was the mental state of his elderly father. During one of their visits they found he hadn't opened his post or even eaten properly. Keeping an eye on him wasn't easy, as he lived two hours away. Far from being a relaxing time, Christmas had been a 24-hour-a-day worry that his dad might do something stupid or damage himself. When Andrew took him home on 4 January, he had been so concerned about whether his dad could manage that he had contacted social services to arrange home visits. By the time he returned to work, Andrew was running on empty.

Exhaustion and stress have become almost normal in today's fast-paced working life. When we stand back and think about it, that is hardly surprising. The expectations we put on ourselves are often way beyond what makes sense, yet we find it difficult to step off the treadmill. If something unexpected happens, we have no energy to spare. Caught in a culture of continuous intensity, we are carried along in the crush of life, like tired passengers packed on a tube train in the rush hour.

Both our working and leisure worlds are saturated with electronic images and noise. We exist in a virtual reality world of computers and email, mobile phones demanding attention, online music and video, television adverts and background noise. Tom Sine calls it 'Boom Town' – the media dream world that is subversively reshaping what is normal and acceptable. I need opportunities to distance myself from this cacophony of electronic input, to draw near to the invisible and infinite. Instead of an information revolution, I need a wisdom revelation. For me, slowing down and stepping aside is a discipline of sanity. The pace of work and life makes time with God essential. It is a learned habit that brings greater harmony and peace.

The discipline of solitude and silence is countercultural. Yet the habit of meditation is essential to Christian living. 'There is . . . a time to be silent and a time to speak' (Ecclesiastes 3:7). Solitude is a time when we are confronted with God and with ourselves. We fear that it may be uncomfortable, which is why many people do not do it. Most of the world will do anything to avoid being alone. However, our actual experience of being alone with God is usually positive; we are changed by it. Some things happen when we are in fellowship with the Lord that do not happen if we ignore him in the rush. Solitude with God gives us new insights into ourselves and into the situations in which we work and live. It is a place where wisdom can unfold as dew forms on a flower – in quietness.

We all need to find spiritual pathways that work for us to connect to God. Some find that just being still is all they need. Others find that being outside in nature, or listening to worship music, is a better way. Personality types and preferred pathways differ. It may be that your kind of retreat involves some planned activity and social interaction with others. The key is whether God is pre-eminent in it.

I drive a hybrid petrol-electric car and the engine control system switches to quiet electric power whenever there is an opportunity. In some ways the Christian life should be like that – switching into prayer and connection with God at every opportunity. It should become a habit so well developed that we do it automatically. We can take small timeouts in a busy day – perhaps just taking a break to make a drink. Connecting with God does not have to be a huge deal. To practise the presence of God in the fast lane, we can develop habits – like the hybrid electric car – of switching into quiet mode whenever the opportunity presents itself. We can use reminders at work, like a screensaver, to take advantage of the little solitudes that punctuate our lives. Apparently Susanna Wesley sometimes used to sit down at home and put her apron over her head to signal to her young children that she was taking a few moments to focus on God.

What a difference

Emily was annoyed. It was all very well having specialists and medical experts, but when they didn't talk to each other the nurse was left to pick up the pieces. The last straw was when the doctor's pager had gone off in the middle of talking to her patient. After different input from the physiotherapist and the occupational therapist, she now had an incomplete explanation from the doctor, who had been called away. The patient was totally confused. Emily's irritation was showing in the snappy way she interacted with the other staff, and she knew it.

On the way back to the nurses' station she passed Alexis, who had obviously just come on duty. 'I need a break,' she thought and took a couple of minutes to visit the ladies' room. At least no-one would hassle her in there!

Only in that moment of quiet did she remember that she had missed taking any time out with God. As she prayed, the realization of her growing anger and the need for forgiveness hit her. 'Father, I can't do this without you,' she sighed. Finally, after asking to be refilled with the Spirit to express patience, kindness and care, Emily wiped her eyes and went back to work a different nurse.

Our motivation to relate to God flows from his grace. Welcoming warmth and a loving relationship with our Father are the hallmarks of a good time out with God. Since there is no condemnation for those who are in Christ Jesus, missing a quiet time is not a punishable offence, but a missed opportunity. I have found that God is very gracious in answering quick prayers, but in the long run I am more blessed by spending extended times in his presence. Relational quality time is usually quantity time.

I used to think that spending time with God was a route to greater effectiveness and fruitfulness and, to be honest, that was my main motivation. Now I realize that practising the presence of God in rest and in work is not just the route, it is also the destination. As the Westminster Confession puts it, 'The chief end of man is to glorify God and enjoy him forever.'

> One thing I ask of the LORD,
>   this is what I seek:
> that I may dwell in the house of the LORD
>   all the days of my life,
> to gaze upon the beauty of the LORD
>   and to seek him in his temple.
> (Psalm 27:4)

Spending extended time alone with God becomes even more vital when we need to make choices. Jesus scheduled his own retreats. Before choosing his disciples, he spent a night alone with his Father praying. On other occasions, he would go off by himself to commune with God and seek his will. The perfect man chose a rhythm of relating to God, who has designed us with a need for him that nothing else will satisfy. That is why taking time out with God is a vital principle for better integration in work and life. Connecting with God is a healthy pattern seasonally, weekly, daily and moment by moment.

Insight Capture Questions
1. When could I take a time out with God?
2. What patterns of solitude might I be able to develop?

17. SANCTUARY

Come with me by yourselves to a quiet place and get some rest.

(Mark 6:31)

Meeting God

Six weeks later, Andrew turned into the gates of a Benedictine monastery at 9.30 a.m. He had set seven hours aside to spend with God. The monk on reception directed him to a room and, almost as an afterthought, said in parting, 'You will be most welcome to join us for the lunchtime singing.'

The confirmation of his dad's Alzheimer's had changed everything. Now he faced a difficult decision. He sat there for a minute or two in silence and suddenly felt very tired. Determined not to fall asleep, he got up to make a coffee. Deciding whether to apply to have his father sectioned under the Mental Health Act felt like playing God. Andrew was very uncomfortable about something so irreversible that would take away his dad's independence. Yet he could see that his ability to take responsibility was already going. He wondered what he would feel like if his own children applied to have him sectioned.

Earlier he had been encouraged when he opened his devotional and read the verse, 'Whether you turn to the right or to the left, your ears will hear a voice behind you, saying, "This is the way; walk in it" ' (Isaiah 30:21). It was a cold, sunny day and a light breeze was blowing over the fields. Andrew went for a walk for about two or three miles, pausing occasionally, looking for something that might give him some sense of clarity. As he wandered along, he heard no voice and he had no sense of peace. Returning to his room, he opened the Bible and after praying scanned the Gospels looking for examples of people who had become incapacitated. He had been here for three hours already and was no further forward. He paced back and forth and prayed for God to show him something.

The bell rang for the regular lunchtime devotions. Feeling at an impasse, he decided to join them. There were only eight monks, arranged in two rows of four, facing each other across the large domed sanctuary. Andrew was given a book so that he could follow the words and he sat in a choir stall as they began. There was a remote, timeless quality about the echoing cadences as the monks sang the liturgy. After a while Andrew stopped following the words and closed his eyes as he felt a sudden peace and the presence of God. In the rhythm of the singing, as if seeing something for the first time, Andrew realized that in his distress he was seeking permission from God. As the singing continued, tears began to roll down his face, as he knew the deep certainty of what he must do, and the assurance that God would take care of it.

A sanctuary does not have to be a monastery, but sometimes we need places to go where God sustains us. We have too much to deal with and are beyond our own capability. During these times we most need God to give us inner peace and reassurance. Even outside times of crisis, Christians have a tendency to get into overload with voluntary activity as well as paid work. It can be helpful to get away for a while and reflect before God on what he is really calling us to do.

That overload is one of the difficulties we face in stepping aside to be with God. Making the time can be a real struggle. I remember the very first time I went on a retreat. After unpacking a few things, praying briefly and reading Scripture, I relaxed and suddenly realized I was incredibly tired. Sitting in a chair in complete quiet, I just fell asleep for two hours. It was the first clear message God gave me on retreat: 'Paul, you are too tired!'

Another difficulty is feeling a failure at prayer. I found this very helpful quote from Brother Lawrence: 'For many years I was bothered by the thought that I was a failure at prayer. Then one day I realized I would always be a failure at prayer; and I've got along better ever since.' I have come to realize that it is not my ability that determines spiritual 'success', it is my availability. It is when I make myself available to God that he begins to connect with me. My choice is to create a space where God can reach me. So, spending time with God is not part of an achievement-centred spirituality, it is a recognition that I need something I cannot get from this world. My life is like a balloon. If I blow up a balloon with as much energy as I can muster and tie a knot in it, no matter how large I make the balloon it still drifts down to the ground, because it is only filled with my breath. If I go to a place where I can fill the balloon with helium, it will rise. In a sense, spending time with God is like getting helium in my balloon. It enables my life to rise in a way I cannot manage on my own.

It can take quite a while to calm the mind. As we unwind, we process and unleash things that have come into our lives.

Thoughts of anger may reveal a need to forgive someone, where we need to engage our heart as well as our will. Remembrances of sin may prompt us to confess and repent. We do not seek to empty our minds or have a kind of nothingness as our 'Nirvana'. No, we seek to fill our minds with Christ. He is the object of our devotion and the means by which we order our thoughts. If something unhelpful suddenly arises, for example some kind of fantasy, we can bring thoughts like that to God in prayer and destroy them in the name of Jesus. 'We demolish arguments and every pretension that sets itself up against the knowledge of God, and we take captive every thought to make it obedient to Christ' (2 Corinthians 10:5). Many helpful patterns have been developed for prayer and time with God. The best one is, of course, the Lord's Prayer, which is a means of focusing on God and his kingdom first, before moving on to our own needs and the needs of others.

Along with many others, I have found that keeping a journal is a helpful means of benefiting from time with God. As we daily read Scripture and pray, things come into our minds that we want to capture – insights we want to retain, perspectives we want to record. I keep a spiral-bound plain book available and write down things occasionally. When I look back in these journals, spanning many years, it is interesting to see how God has moved in my life. Some things only make sense later. For example, while praying during the day on 11 February 1995, I had a strong impression of the word 'Trees'. Now this could have been a figment of my imagination or a random idea that had no bearing on anything. Nevertheless, I wrote it down in my journal. To my surprise, I then found that the evening reading for 11 February started with this verse: 'The trees of the LORD are well watered' (Psalm 104:16), and the reading continued on the theme of trees. How do you explain that? I could not understand why God might be drawing my attention to trees, but it did prompt me to do a Bible study on trees and fruitfulness. That helped me understand how spiritual formation and transformation is a process similar to trees developing and bearing fruit. As it is written:

> He is like a tree planted by streams of water,
>   which yields its fruit in season
> and whose leaf does not wither.
> (Psalm 1:3)

Helping people grow in discipleship and fruitfulness has turned out to be an emerging theme in my life.

Time out with God is something that benefits us when planned in certain rhythms. The weekly Sabbath is the obvious example. Some years ago I read about a biblical day starting in the evening, 'And there was evening and there was morning, the first day' (Genesis 1:5), and since then I have been taking my weekly 24 hours off starting in the evening. I found it to be a better pattern – easier to unwind in the evening and sleep more deeply. Since I naturally start thinking about the following day during the previous evening, I find that the end of my day off is a good time to plan.

Legalism is a risk with any spiritual discipline. The Sabbath is for our well-being, not to bind us with an unbreakable rule. 'The Sabbath was made for people, not people for the Sabbath' (Mark 2:27 NIVI). God wants us to benefit from rhythms of rest. We may also find that more extended times of reflection are helpful as seasons of our lives change, when we can pray and ponder on our work and life with a longer perspective.

Insight Capture Questions
1. What issue might benefit from an extended time of prayer and meditation?
2. Where could I record more of my spiritual journey?

18. MOVING ON?

I will walk about in freedom,
for I have sought out your precepts.
(Psalm 119:45)

No way out

She thought about resigning, but it would wreck any possibility of a comeback. She thought about joining competitors, but that would be geographically difficult while her husband's job stayed the same. She even considered legal action, but dismissed it. All her career credibility was with this employer. Stella did not know what to do, and she felt trapped.

Having returned to work as a full-time actuary after taking time off when her first child was born, Stella had quickly been assigned to help manage the pension fund of a large company. It was a great opportunity and to begin with she especially enjoyed the client meetings, as the management were exploring a change in pension plan design.

However, one day a client meeting was rescheduled from 2 p.m. to 4 p.m. and she had to arrange additional childcare cover. It was the beginning of a regular pattern. She started to find the timing of meetings awkward – sometimes not getting away until well past 6 p.m. Stella hated getting home when her young son was asleep and although she discussed it with her boss, he was reluctant to inconvenience the client. She began to wonder whether returning to work had been the right thing. The culture at work was to stay late. Soon she found she was getting home after Johnnie's bedtime two or three nights a week.

Stella asked her boss about part-time work. He was sympathetic, but could not assign her to clients on a part-time basis. A part-time job would mean a back-office role. Already struggling with guilt at leaving her child during the day, now Stella had to deal with anger too and found herself having to forgive everyone – the client, her boss, her child, and most of all herself. A back-office role was not her choice and she knew that a step back from customer responsibility after such a short time would irritate the client and embarrass her boss. There seemed no way out of a situation in which either her family or her career would be compromised.

Our choice of job is a very important aspect of integrating work and life, yet it is something on which the Bible seems to say very little. For most of history, the majority of jobs involved hunting, farming, agriculture or basic trades, and they were jobs for life. Today we live with a bewildering new array of specialized jobs in a global economy where job security is transient. Greater mobility coupled with advanced technology and communications have opened up more working possibilities and altered the pattern of many careers to one of frequent change. What principles in Scripture might help us to navigate through this different environment?

Changing job involves risk and going into the unknown. It is a part of the journey of faith for the Christian. When

God called Israel to go on a journey from Egypt to Canaan, he gave them freedom while commanding the same people to stay within geographic and moral limits. So it is with the believer's journey of faith through the job market. It is a journey of faith needing the wisdom and obedience to keep within limits.

Each of us has freedom and limits in our work life. When we are employed, we usually have the freedom to make some decisions and the authority to manage things within our delegated area of responsibility. We also have limits and we need to know what those limits are and stay within them. Both the freedom we enjoy and the limits we observe are under God's authority and his authorities at work. 'The authorities that exist have been established by God' (Romans 13:1).

God's limits are mainly to do with relationships and well-being. The moral law is a set of limits designed to protect our relationships and keep our communities and ourselves in good health. Relationships involve limits. Everybody else's life puts a limitation on my life, and those who are closest to me limit me the most. Children are a limitation, parents are a limitation and spouses are a limitation. These people are not minor inconveniences: they impose major respon-sibilities and constraints on what I can and cannot do. Relationships are more important than autonomy or achieve-ment and relationships rightly put important limits on our choice of job.

Sometimes God gives people a very specific call (mon-archs, priests, prophets, apostles and pastors are examples) and that puts limits on their working life. For most of us, though, our calling is something we discover over time and choosing a specific job is something where we enjoy freedom under God. That does not mean that finding or doing a job is easy – the ground is cursed because of the fall (Genesis 3:17). Factors such as the economic environment and our own health, capability or availability may make it difficult to get work, but we do have some choice. So we need to be as flexible and creative as possible in making ourselves employable – either as workers in an organization or as self-employed people providing services.

Lateral thinking

Over coffee at church, Stella asked Jean if she would be willing to come round one evening and talk about her job. Jean had worked in human resources in the past. When she arrived at 8 p.m. the following Wednesday, Stella had had a good day. She had been home by 5.30 p.m., bathed her son and chatted to Stan for half an hour.

After they had prayed, Stella unfolded her predicament and Jean nodded sympathetically as Stella explained why she believed it was right to have a limit on her availability for work, because of her responsibility as a wife and mother.

'Well,' Jean said finally, 'the way I see it, something's got to give.'

'Tell me about it!' said Stella.

'Which of these can change?' Jean continued. 'Who you work for, what you do, or where and when you do it – which of those can change?'

'That's just it,' said Stella. 'I don't seem to be able to change any of them without resigning. I can't work for anyone else doing what I'm doing now. I can't move and I can't do this job part time.'

'So could you do a different job?'

'What, in the same company?' asked Stella.

'Sure,' said Jean. 'It's a large organization.'

'But I'm an actuary,' said Stella.

'No, you're a child of God, who happens to be working as an actuary at present. You could do something else.'

Stella opened her hands in despair. 'Like what? I don't have training for other roles.'

'You're a people person, aren't you?' asked Jean.

'I enjoy working with people, yes,' replied Stella.

'So, what role could you have in the organization that would utilize your skills and still allow you to meet people?'

Stella looked blank. 'I don't know.'

'Find out. If you could identify a different role like that, you might be able to do it for a few years and then go back to client contact as an actuary later – if you still wanted to.'

As we explore the freedom God has given us to choose work, there are three main options in job change: (a) who you work for; (b) what you do; and (c) your availability (i.e. where and when you work). I think of these things as being like three axes or boundaries and find it to be a helpful framework (see figure 6). When a person is changing job, there tends to be tension between how flexible they are willing to be and the flexibility that is needed to keep being employable.

In the long run, crossing these boundaries is often a good thing, because it leads to greater learning and experience and often to greater employability. However, everyone finds new things challenging, so trying to change everything at

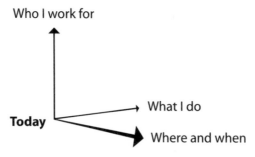

Figure 6. Options in job change

once may be unwise. A pragmatic approach is to try to fix one axis and let the others float. In that way we may be able to keep some aspects of our lives that we do not want to change and still find opportunity to work. If we have not heard a specific call from God regarding our job, then these general principles may help us to make a sensible choice.

Early in my career, my employer merged with another company and my wife and I did not want to live where they were based. At the time I was working as a management accountant, so I looked for another management accounting job with a new employer in a different location. (That was fixing the 'what I do' axis.) After we had moved, we became committed Christians, found a good church community and believed God was guiding us to stay in the same place. So as opportunities arose, I tried to fix the geographic ('availability') axis and let the 'who I work for' and 'what I do' axes float. The result was that I moved into different divisions and functions of the company where I had no previous experience. I consider myself very fortunate to have had these opportunities in a large organization willing to take a risk on me because of my previous track record with them. In this way, I was able to continue working in the same geographic area for the following twenty years. In the final five years of my career I was able to change my working pattern to put an extra day a week into the local church.

Insight Capture Questions
1. Which of the three axes of freedom would I choose to fix if I could?
2. If I changed job, what boundaries could I choose to cross?

19. FINDING A FIT

Do you see those who are skilled in their work?
They will serve before kings.
(Proverbs 22:29 NIVI)

New dimension

Stella was over the moon. Jean had been right. There was another way. Stella now worked fixed hours in a job with customers using her actuarial skills in the same company. What she thought had been impossible had been achieved. She had been granted a two-year secondment to a part-time role delivering specialized training to various groups who needed technical expertise, like pension fund trustees. It was not a job with account responsibility, but Stella could live with different customers for a while. It had been a step of faith, because she had never done training before, but she found she enjoyed it. Her new responsibility gave her the people dimension she sought at work and enabled her to give the commitment she wanted to her family.

Each of us has to manage our particular mix of work, family, church and other relational responsibilities alongside our jobs. The right choice for one person in one situation may be the wrong choice for a different person in a similar situation, because our lives are not the same. This is where personal prayer, seeking the guidance of God and discussing our limits with the people closest to us are wise actions to take.

As we reflect on how well we fit our jobs, I have found the following framework to be a useful way to analyse the overlap between a person and an organization. The model works for paid or voluntary jobs, manual or knowledge work, and for self-employed people relating to customers and partners. The individual and the organization are represented by two triangles that overlap at various levels – the greater the overlap, the more key it is to employability.

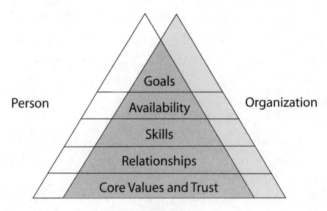

Figure 7. Checking my fit with the job

The order in which these overlapping qualities are stacked in this picture can change depending on their importance to both the organization and the individual. The order I have shown reflects my belief that matching core values and healthy relationships are often the most critical areas for long-term employability. In Stella's case, the availability overlap was the presenting issue. For others it may be a skills gap, or a blocked development path.

Thinking about issues in this way enables us to reflect on

the following questions as we think about the fit with existing or potential jobs.

- How well do my personal values match the core values of the organization?
- Do I know people in the organization with whom I have healthy relationships and empathy?
- Are my skills and competencies a good match for the work?
- How well does the likely pattern of the job fit my availability?
- Are my personal goals for growth consistent with what the organization wants?

All job change is either reactive or proactive. Mostly it is reactive, as it was with Stella. Circumstances change and we need to make a change. The change trigger may be a problem with working hours, or our skills becoming obsolete with new technology, or organizational restructuring that can suddenly eliminate a job. Navigating through a reactive job change can be a difficult and stressful experience, but it can also be a time of personal growth when God strengthens our faith. Many people who have been suddenly forced into a job change through redundancy have said that, looking back, it was one of the best things that happened to them, the nudge they needed to cross a boundary they would never otherwise have attempted.

Rob Harley told me how the Bee Gees got started. The brothers used to do karaoke in Manchester theatres. Then one day they accidentally broke the records they used for the backing tracks just before they were due to go on stage. In fear and trepidation, they decided to 'wing it' and sang on their own – and discovered the Bee Gees! They found they did not need the backing track as security. Sometimes our existing jobs are like old backing tracks that slow our growth.

One reason why a proactive change of job may be advisable is in order to move closer to our vocation – the sense of divine call in our life. An example would be someone discovering over time that their true vocation is selling. Perhaps they enjoy relating with people to understand their needs. Gaining commitment from others is something that comes naturally. Gradually it becomes clear that selling is what they were made to do. Moving to selling could be difficult, because of short-term training needs or pay differences, but it would be a change that would be likely to produce better fulfilment and fruitfulness in their lives.

Another reason for a job change might be to move geographically closer to extended family, to improve the care and mutual support structure. Or we may decide to go self-employed in order to alter our availability for others. These are relational motivators.

Ambition, wealth, power and status are all motivations that we need to recognize and be careful about. We may be offered promotion at work and that is often a good thing, a sign of both competence and trust. Christians in key positions of influence in organizations can be a strategic advantage in the kingdom of God. When I was being interviewed for more senior positions in my career, I found it nearly impossible to disentangle all my mixed motives and used to pray that God would bless me and block me from getting the job if it was the wrong thing for me.

Below are some of the questions we may find helpful to ask ourselves when considering a job change.

- How will a job change affect my relationship commitments?

- Will this new job responsibility give me the opportunity to do what I do best?
- What are the opinions of the key people in my life?
- Can I bring more glory to God through changing my job, or by staying in my current job?

We can get overly anxious about trying to find the 'exact' job that God has for us. Other than the historical fact that most people in the past did what their parents did, perhaps one reason why the Bible says little about choosing a job is that God is more interested in developing our character. It is the way we do our job that is more important than the job itself.

Not many of us have the luxury of having a job we enjoy all the time. Debra Veal, the woman who rowed the Atlantic alone after her husband and rowing partner fell ill, had to face months of monotonous and backbreaking rowing. She hung a sign in her cabin that said, 'Choose your attitude.' Every day it was a reminder that we might not be able to choose what we have to do, but we can choose our attitude towards doing it.

> Whatever you do, work at it with all your heart, as working
> for the Lord, not for human masters, since you know that
> you will receive an inheritance from the Lord as a reward. It
> is the Lord Christ you are serving.
> (Colossians 3:23–24 NIVI)

Insight Capture Questions
1. How well do I fit my current job?
2. What is my usual working attitude?

20. WHAT DO YOU REALLY WANT?

Show me your ways, O LORD,
    teach me your paths;
guide me in your truth and teach me,
    for you are God my Saviour,
    and my hope is in you all day long.
(Psalm 25:4–5)

Decisions decisions

The train was packed and that curious awkwardness of social isolation in close proximity filled the carriage. Above the noise of the train a couple could be heard discussing the pros and cons of moving house. Pradeep was poring over some literature from a company that had been at his graduate recruitment fair, wondering whether to apply. Ben was staring out of the window thinking about whether to propose to his girlfriend. Behind him, Janet was considering changing her job and was browsing a magazine, hoping that her horoscope would give some clear direction. Suddenly a mobile phone started to ring and there was universal irritation amongst all those pondering major decisions, as the offender started talking about the trivia of her day.

Some folk were fortunate enough to be sitting down. Having recently had a scan, Nigel was concerned about a possible tumour and was feeling unsure about how much to communicate to his boss. Kam Leung had a copy of *The Economist* open, though he wasn't reading it. Instead he was wondering whether to sell the business he had built up over the last ten years and go back to Hong Kong. Derek was wondering how he was going to manage until payday and whether he should draw some cash at the station.

So many people today are looking for guidance. It is said that if one of the seminar options at a conference is on guidance, about half of the delegates will select it – no matter how many other alternatives there are. At a recent event I attended for Christian business people, half of them named their top issue as understanding God's will for the next step in their lives. People seek guidance for various reasons. Some are seeking a general understanding of their calling and direction for life. Others are agonizing over a specific choice, such as a change of job or career.

A typical modern-day approach to making decisions is first to consult something like the internet, or perhaps a self-help book or magazine. Then, having gathered some information and opinions, the next step is to think about the options and finally make a choice. God is not part of the process. Society's normal pattern matches the culture in the book of Judges where the last verse of the book says, 'In those days Israel had no king; everyone did as they saw fit' (Judges 21:25 NIVI).

Even those who know God can often substitute something else for God when it comes to making decisions. If we choose what *we* think is best, we are using a method based on predicted outcome and self-interest. Os Hillman calls this the 'Greek Model' of guidance. It is weighing up the pros and cons, an intellectual method that makes our reasoning ability our god. The Bible has a rather blunt comment on this approach: 'Those who trust in themselves are fools' (Proverbs 28:26 NIVI).

Being properly briefed on making choices is wise. God has given us minds and it is good and right to use them, but if we trust only our own assessment we are likely to run into trouble. Examples of forgetting the God dimension of guidance litter Scripture. People made decisions that looked sensible, but they were deceived because they did not enquire of God. Abraham and Sarah decided to use Hagar as a surrogate mother with difficult long-term consequences (Genesis 16). Joshua and the Israelites were deceived into making a treaty with the Gibeonites, again resulting in a long-term problem (Joshua 9). These examples show the negative results of only trusting our own reasoning.

Instinctively we know that there is something missing in the purely rational approach. We feel the need for a deeper level of assurance. We want to know God's will, or at the very least have the reassurance that we are not outside his will. Our mental reasoning is incomplete without this heart-felt conviction.

One man approached me at the end of a conference session and asked my opinion on whether he should sell his business – a potentially huge decision where some prayer and fasting might well have been a wise course of action. The man hardly knew me and I sensed real anxiety as he searched to know the right thing to do. When I asked him how much time he had spent on his own praying about it, he said that coming to the Christian conference was the time he had allocated for the decision. I had the impression that he was going from one session to another, desperately hoping that one of the speakers would give him a divine answer. This is a dangerous way to make a decision.

Christians have personal promises from God of being able to hear his voice, just as sheep hear and know the voice of their shepherd.

> . . . his sheep follow him because they know his voice . . .
> I am the good shepherd; I know my sheep and my sheep know me.
> (John 10:4, 14)

> I will instruct you and teach you in the way you should go;
>> I will counsel you and watch over you.
> (Psalm 32:8)

Yet in practice we find it hard to hear from God, often because we are too focused on other things rather than listening to him.

On the high slopes of the Colorado mountains, blind skiers wearing red outfits are accompanied by skiing instructors who call out to them. What do you think is the most important thing to those blind skiers? The voice of their instructor. When we get to a place where the guidance of God is of supreme importance in our lives, we will seek him with real intensity – the same kind of listening intensity that blind skiers have in needing to hear their instructor.

How much do I really want to know God and seek his will? What choices am I prepared to make to give me the best possible opportunity to hear God's voice?

When we know someone very well, we can often predict their reaction to a suggestion we might make. After over thirty years of marriage, I do not always need to ask my wife Helen about her preferences, because I often know what they are – and she knows the same about me. We know with reasonable accuracy what the other's opinion will be on a lot of issues. In the same way, if you live in a close relationship with God, you get to know what he thinks about a lot of things. So when something comes up, you are in a much better position to know his opinion.

Getting to know someone is not an exact science. Some ways are obvious, such as conversation, but not everything is disclosed in conversation. New situations in life and joint experiences can give new insights into someone. Helen and I are still discovering things about each other, even after all this time. It is a bit like that with getting to know God.

All relationships need time. In an earlier chapter, taking regular time with God was discussed as an important means of growing in our relationship with him. During these times we can study the Bible and pray. We can engage in the spiritual disciplines of confession and repentance, which remove blockages in our relationship with God. We can reflect on our lifestyles and choose gradually to eliminate things that are hindering our intimacy with him. It takes growth and maturity to make these changes. The best way to hear God is in the context of a pattern of living in close communion with him.

Willing slave?

The thought of being promoted to work for a man he knew was a hardened workaholic was frightening. Being General Manager of the subsidiary would also mean more travel, especially to headquarters in Japan, and longer hours. He would probably have to do more 'corporate entertaining' of large clients. It was definitely outside his comfort zone. What really bugged him, though, was that when he prayed about it, God seemed to be encouraging him.

It would be a first for a local national to hold the position of General Manager, a sign of trust. The phrase 'making the most of every opportunity, because the days are evil' (Ephesians 5:16) leapt out at him from his Bible reading. He had asked advice from one of the church leaders who, after praying with him, smiled and said, 'The Lord is with you, mighty warrior!' (Judges 6:12) His wife pointed out that he would have greater influence to create a working climate more closely matched with his Christian values.

God seemed to be giving him green lights everywhere, but part of him just felt like running away.

Unfortunately, guidance from God may not always be what we want to hear. He has a habit of taking us outside our comfort zones. If I do hear God, am I really willing to do what he says?

> The word of the LORD came to Jonah son of Amittai: 'Go to the great city of Nineveh and preach against it, because its wickedness has come up before me.'
> But Jonah ran away from the LORD and headed for Tarshish. (Jonah 1:1–3)

George Müller wrote:

> I seek at the beginning to get my heart into such a state that it has no will of its own in regard to a given matter. Nine tenths of the trouble with people generally is just here. Nine tenths of the difficulties are overcome when our hearts are ready to do the knowledge of what his will is.

A. W. Tozer said that the man or woman who is 'joyously surrendered' to Christ cannot make a wrong choice – any choice will be the right one.

One of the most penetrating questions Jesus asked others in the Gospels was, 'What do you want me to do for you?' Well, what do you really want from God? If we genuinely seek guidance, we have to face two heart-searching questions:

- How much do I really want to hear God?
- When I do hear him, am I willing to do what he says?

> Insight Capture Questions
> 1. What decision am I facing now where I may be leaving God out?
> 2. What may be hindering my ability to hear from God?

21. COMMON SENSE?

We have the word of the prophets made more certain, and you will do well to pay attention to it, as to a light shining in a dark place.

(2 Peter 1:19)

The whole truth?

The old man was quite badly bruised and the explanation of it being caused by a fall was questionable. Now the man's family had contacted a newspaper and Ian had half an hour before a reporter arrived at the local council offices for an interview. Although there was no previous history of abuse, Ian knew that this council-supervised care home was short staffed. He realized how old folk can sometimes be difficult and wondered what had really happened. As soon as there was a whiff of press interest, the Chief Executive's office had phoned him with some strong advice not to say anything that would make the political leadership look inept.

As a Christian he wasn't going to lie; his issue was how much of the truth to tell. On the one hand, there was clearly a problem with inadequate resources in social services. On the other hand, how much was it really in the public interest to have the whole incident splashed over the papers? What should he say?

The issue of selective disclosure seemed to keep recurring in his job. Where did discretion end and concealment begin? Some politicians spun the truth for their own reasons, but as a Christian and a public servant he found that kind of pressure very uncomfortable.

Ethical dilemmas at work are quite common. They can range from issues such as 'small white lies' to the brutal suppression of truth and justice. Working in organizations almost always involves coming up against an ethical issue at some stage.

If only it were possible to look up the exact situation we face on page three zillion of the Bible and get a clear answer! Unfortunately it is not possible. Maybe that is a good thing, because the way God guides us is not with legalism, but with the living Word. Instead of giving us an index to every possibility in work and life, we are given principles and an interpreter. The genius of Scripture is that we can study it through the lens of our own story and find timeless truths that apply to us all.

One of the biggest problems most believers have in knowing God's guidance is not knowing his Word. Christians who spend time in the Bible are more likely to hear God's voice clearly and accurately. Those who study the Word and really take the trouble to think about what it means personally, equip themselves to understand God's will. When a life situation arises, scripture relating to that topic often comes to mind. God's wisdom in his Word is brought to bear on a specific decision by the Holy Spirit, and we are guided.

The unfolding of your words gives light . . .
Your word is a lamp to my feet
    and a light for my path.
(Psalm 119:130, 105)

Brief times of looking at a daily devotional – valuable though they are for strengthening, encouragement and comfort – may not have sufficient intensity or duration to transform us. It is like the difference between a snack and a meal. Transformation by the renewing of our minds through Scripture is best done with a measure of uninterrupted focus. When we really engage with a passage of Scripture, studying it for ourselves, unpacking the meaning and praying it into our lives, then we begin to change.

The Bible reveals what is sometimes called God's general will. For example:

> Your Father in heaven is not willing that any of these little ones should be lost.
> (Matthew 18:14)

> My Father's will is that all those who look to the Son and believe in him shall have eternal life, and I will raise them up at the last day.
> (John 6:40 NIVI)

From this it follows that a universal right choice for every single human being is to receive Jesus as Saviour and Lord and follow him. That is God's general will. All other Christian choices in life must fit within the context of that general will. It is also God's general will that we should be holy. It is written, 'Be holy, because I am holy' (1 Peter 1:16). There are many other examples.

God's general will provides us with guidelines that help us understand his specific will. Often we want guidance on a specific issue, but we have not spent time understanding the will of God generally. Our tendency to avoid taking personal responsibility can make us susceptible to looking for exceptional 'supernatural' guidance that absolves us of the need to think.

After a seminar, a lady came up to me and asked my opinion about whether she should marry an Indian doctor! She hardly knew me – I was just somebody who happened to be speaking at the event. The frightening thing is that if I had expressed a strong opinion, I feel it would have impacted her decision significantly. When I asked whether this Indian doctor was a believer, she said she was not sure. So I asked what her reaction was to the scripture that begins, 'Do not be yoked together with unbelievers' (2 Corinthians 6:14–18). She was obviously already painfully aware of this, and I began to wonder whether she just wanted someone to give her permission to do something she already suspected was against the will of God.

Unfortunately, this is quite common. Natural selfish desires can often lead us towards things that are outside the general will of God. No matter how much we want to get permission to do them, there is no getting away from the fact that God's will sets general limits. If we step outside these limits, then we are stepping outside the will of God. It is definitely outside the will of God to view pornography. It is definitely outside the will of God to embezzle money. The Ten Commandments set all kinds of limits, not with an angry tone of voice, but with a loving concern from a gracious God who does not want us to be damaged.

Within these general limits there is a freedom to choose and this is where we can sometimes get overly concerned. Some see God's will like a tightrope and fear putting a foot wrong. This can be a form of perfectionism and shows a distorted understanding of God's character. Our Father is not a nitpicker who makes us suffer unless our choices are perfect. He gives us a lot of freedom. Rob Parsons gives an example of a man who, after praying about which of two job opportunities he should choose, got an answer from God: 'You choose, either one is fine with me!'

Part of the general will of God is that we exercise choice within his limits. He has given us the capability and freedom to make decisions in a godly way. That is not a licence for ignoring him or being disobedient, but a plea to trust our Father even if we make a mistake. I have made many mistakes in my life, yet by the grace and mercy of God, I am still here. I do not want to be foolish or irresponsible, but sometimes we need to lighten up a bit and give God some credit for still being in overall control.

It is good to remember that we are not alone in our decision making. The body of Christ, the gathered community of believers to whom we belong in the local church, is a great resource. That does not mean that every time we face a choice we go round asking everybody what they think. But God does communicate with us through other Christians and he uses the relationships we have with other believers to help guide us in life. This is an element of guidance that is very often ignored or minimized in our individualistic world. I would never recommend that a final decision is made just on the basis of what somebody else says, but it does make sense to consult with others who know us before a decision is reached.

Plans fail for lack of counsel,
    but with many advisers they succeed.
(Proverbs 15:22)

The body of Christ can provide a broad consensus and confirmation of what God is saying to us. Sometimes a situation develops where we are torn in two or more directions. Maybe we are confronted with multiple opportunities, or perhaps we have conflicting duties – for example, when the care of someone who is ill or disabled conflicts with the responsibilities we have at work. Richard Foster points out that guidance is a corporate discipline. That does not mean that we take democratic votes on what to do, but others can help us see if we are deluding ourselves or being driven by selfishness or guilt.

Although the church is fallible and its leaders are fallible, nevertheless God still uses both to provide mentoring and confirmation of his will to individual believers. If we are not part of a church, we deny ourselves an important channel of assistance. People who are unwilling to check their decisions with others are in a dangerous place. If our choices are secretive and our attitude is brittle, it is unlikely that we are submitted to God. How can we submit to God if we cannot submit to anyone else?

An overwhelming desire of the heart of Jesus is for unity amongst his followers. This unity is the ultimate testimony of the presence of God and it is partly why Christians seek the advice and confirmation of other believers. There is great assurance and strengthening if a Christian is affirmed by people in the wider church for what God is calling them to do. The Word of God, the Spirit of God and the people of God resonate. Agreement between them is an extremely powerful thing.

Insight Capture Questions
1. What am I doing regularly to study and apply the Bible to my work and life?
2. Who are the people I ask for prayer and advice when I face an important decision?

22. SPIRITED CONVICTION

My conscience confirms it in the Holy Spirit.
(Romans 9:1)

Tough love

Becky stared out of the train window at the endless
scenery. Glancing at her watch, she closed her eyes.
Only another twenty minutes to go. It had not been a
good day. The harsh, critical words of her boss kept
repeating themselves over and over in her head, trig-
gering the painful memory of her husband's desertion.
She tried to think of something else, but her mind
veered back to it like a magnetized needle. Anger at the
way she had been treated and fear of losing her job
washed over her in waves. There was no-one to share it
with. She would have to swallow the pain, pick up the
children and try not to snap at them before they went
to bed. She knew she needed time alone with God.

Thankfully they settled well and she had some
time on her own. Half an hour later, Becky got up
from her knees and dried her eyes. Forgiveness had
not been easy and she felt drained, but at peace.
Wandering into the kitchen and opening the fridge,
she found a chocolate yoghurt. Perhaps she should
look for another job, but would she get one that paid
enough or gave her the flexibility she needed for the
children? Did she have the energy to start looking?
She checked on her sleeping children, finished clearing up, and went wearily to bed.

At three o'clock the following morning she was suddenly awake and didn't know why. She lay there quietly listening, but could sense nothing except her own heartbeat. Switching on the light, Becky sat up and out of sheer habit picked up a devotional book on her bedside table. Opening it at that day's date, she read:

> The LORD your God is with you,
>   he is mighty to save.
> He will take great delight in you,
>   he will quiet you with his love,
>   he will rejoice over you with singing.
> (Zephaniah 3:17)

She knew it was God. As the power of that Word spoke into her heart, she knew that she didn't have to let her boss's criticism define her. There was someone who loved her more than that. She would stay with her job and even her boss. God's grace was enough.

The Word of God is interpreted by the Spirit of God. 'We have not received the spirit of the world but the Spirit who is from God, that we may understand what God has freely given us' (1 Corinthians 2:12). We can ask God for the wisdom and fullness of his Spirit! He is very clear that he longs to answer such a prayer (Luke 11:13). 'Why is it,' asks comedienne Lily Tomlin, 'that when we speak to God we are said to be praying, but if God speaks to us we are said to be schizophrenic?' It makes sense that he has given us the means – the Holy Spirit – to discern his voice and to know his will. It is the Holy

Spirit who helps us to hear and recognize God's personal Word to us in what is preached and what is written.

God can also make himself known in and through our thoughts and perceptions. The Holy Spirit searches our hearts and minds and is intimately involved with our thoughts and the process of developing a conviction about the right way to go. Proverbs 20:27 says:

> The lamp of the LORD searches the human spirit;
>   it searches out the inmost being.
>
> (NIVI)

Or, in another translation:

> The spirit of man is the candle of the LORD,
>   searching all the inward parts of the belly.
>
> (AV)

In other words, the Spirit of God helps us get to the guts of the issue.

How do we know that this inner voice is God, as opposed to just ourselves, or even the devil? After all, don't mental patients, maniacs and terrorists claim to hear voices telling them to do things? Isn't it all too easy to interpret the things we read or hear through the lens of our own emotions or our own preferences? We get so many distractions from within ourselves and from the world around us.

One answer is that the voice of God has a different and definite quality about it. Dallas Willard writes that 'God's voice has a serene weight, a unique spirit . . . [and this is critical] a content consistent with Scripture'. It takes diligence and experience to both listen to and learn to recognize God's voice. It takes practice and that means sometimes making mistakes, which is why we should avoid being dogmatic. For those who keep a journal, looking back at what we have recorded sometimes helps us to see patterns in what God may be saying to us over a period of time.

The Bible speaks of a personal conviction which is subjective. It is called 'knowing'. Our word 'knowing' is normally associated with factual or technical knowledge, but there is a deeper kind of knowing something. The first letter of John uses the phrase 'we know' sixteen times, and the meaning is one of an inner certainty in the context of a faith in God: an inner personal conviction and divine agreement, powerfully convicting our mind, heart and will – our whole being.

As we search for the inner conviction that God is developing in us, sometimes it finds an outlet in what we ourselves say to others. I have often observed that people who speak out things to others are, in fact, speaking what God is saying to them. As a preacher, I find God's word to me is often the word spoken by me. Even in casual conversation, people sometimes reveal what God is forming in their hearts. 'Out of the overflow of the heart the mouth speaks' (Matthew 12:34). Could it be that what you have been saying to others, God is in fact saying to you?

Think about how Jesus was guided. The Gospels show Jesus taking time out to be with his Father and developing quiet conviction about what he should do next. As I mentioned in an earlier chapter, we see Jesus going off to be alone early in the morning and then, after a time spent with God, saying, 'I must preach the good news of the kingdom of God to the other towns also, because that is why I was sent' (Luke 4:43). We do not know exactly how he developed this conviction about which course to take, but we do know that it flowed from his time with God. Another example is his night of prayer before the critical selection of the twelve apostles. We do not see God guiding Jesus in dramatic ways. We see the quiet working out of choices in his heart in communion with his Father.

My story

In September 1992 our minister resigned after five years of ill health and a number of weary folk left the church. Just a few committed families remained in a very small, struggling congregation of only fourteen adult members, some of whom were elderly. It was a time of great discouragement and uncertainty. I was church secretary at the time, but was unsure whether it was right for my family to stay, or even whether the church should continue in its existing form.

Our two boys were aged twelve and eight – ages when young people often begin to drift away from church. In the morning service, when the time came for the children to leave for their classes, there were just two boys going out – my younger son, and the youngest son of the church treasurer. I remember being grateful for the dedication of the lady teaching them and at the same time wondering whether this situation would really be helpful for the spiritual development of our family.

My wife and I both resolved to pray and seek God's will. I went into a time of prayer and fasting and one night I had an unusual dream of my house being surrounded by a firestorm. I found myself wide awake in the early hours of the morning – very unusual for me as I normally sleep like a log. I got up, went downstairs, opened my Bible and was leafing through it when I came across the passage in 1 Kings 19 about

Elijah in the cave. He was discouraged and complaining to God that he felt like the only one left. Somehow, I identified with that!

Elijah looked outside at the fire and the wind, but God was not in them. He was in the still small voice. God commanded Elijah to go back the way he had come and anoint two kings. For Elijah to turn around and go back, he would have to face the very thing he had been running away from, in his case Jezebel. I realized that I was running away from the situation I was in and that God was telling me to turn around and go back the way I had come. In other words, I was to stop thinking about leaving and walk back into my responsibility. I shared this with my wife, who had also developed a conviction from God that we should stay.

Holy Spirit conviction is a strange thing. It sounds arrogant to *know* something in a way that is certain. All I can say is that from the Word of God, and from deep within my heart, came a quiet and complete conviction that I should stay in that church. That did not make the decision easy, but it did give me peace.

Now we can look back and see that it was the right decision. From the time that we decided to stay, the church grew consistently and the morning congregation is now around 150. My sons, about whom I was so worried, are now grown men and both actively involved in the church.

That choice we made had a far-reaching impact, both on our own lives and on the lives of others. It was not directly relevant to my work at the time, but in the long run it affected my choice of job and the decision to stay in the same company, because we knew we should not move out of the area. I wonder what would have happened if I had just followed my own reasoning and fears and walked away? I have a feeling that our family would not have enjoyed so much blessing.

I believe that Holy Spirit conviction is an authentic Christian experience, which is promised by Jesus. 'My sheep listen to my voice; I know them, and they follow me' (John 10:27). We are not infallible, far from it, but we are children of God. We can experience the deep peace of Christ in our heart. We can experience the Holy Spirit interpreting Scripture to us. We can experience agreement together. We can *know* God's will.

Insight Capture Questions
1. Is there a significant choice I have to make where I need real conviction?
2. What will I do to engage with God about it?

PART 3

DEVELOPING PURPOSE

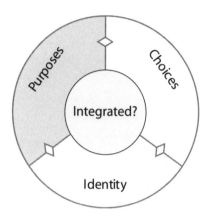

Figure 8

23. WHY AM I HERE?

It is the glory of God to conceal a matter;
  to search out a matter is the glory of kings.
(Proverbs 25:2)

The difference

The small, wizened Albanian woman smiled as she shook the hand of the young princess and went inside for tea. Little did either know that in a short while they would both die within a few days of each other. The crowds who watched had not just come to see a celebrity; they had come to see someone who was a legend in her own lifetime. Nothing about her physical features endeared her to people, yet they flocked to see her and to sense her presence and love. The quality of being anointed by God rested on her and the people knew it. Mother Teresa was a called person.

A called person is mysteriously attractive; their sense of quiet purpose and passion is magnetic. A special energy is released when we do what we were born to do. In the film *Billy Elliot*, a selector at the Royal Ballet asks Billy, 'What do you feel when you dance?' and he replies, 'Electricity, I feel electricity.' That is a sign of someone's 'Factor X', when there is an electric feeling about what we do. Our calling is usually consistent with a sense of passion, an important clue to understanding what God has already put within us. Sometimes athletes refer to exceptional performance as being 'in the zone'. When someone is fulfilling what they were made to do, they are 'in the zone' with that sense of both passion and effectiveness.

Most people want to know the answer to the question, 'How can I be the best person I can possibly be?' It is one of the most popular topics in self-help books today. One of the big mistakes some of these books make is failing to distinguish between discovery and invention. The idea of choosing our own dream and fulfilling it sounds great, but the Bible is clear that it is God who has chosen our dream. 'For we are God's workmanship, created in Christ Jesus to do good works, which God prepared in advance for us to do' (Ephesians 2:10). He has hardwired into our capabilities and motivation both the skills and the passion to fulfil these good works. Our task is to discover what he has done, not invent our own ideas. The younger we are when we engage with the topic the better, because once we begin to see ourselves through the lens of what God has planned for us, we move more purposefully through work and life.

However, we are called first to Christ rather than to any specific role. It is in Christ alone that our core identity is truly found, not in the secondary call to work or vocation. If our work becomes our identity, we are in trouble. 'When a man knows how to do something,' Pablo Picasso told a friend, 'he ceases being a man when he stops doing it.' The result, he said, was a driven man. We are not to be like that.

A personal mission statement is a simple sentence that summarizes God's purpose for your work and life, reflecting your unique passion and sense of focus. Although the aim is a simple summary, it often takes a lot of searching and thought before we can arrive at a statement that others can confirm accurately reflects how God has made us. The benefit of discovering a personal mission is that it infuses work and life with greater focus, enabling us to develop in areas that match our strengths and reduce or eliminate activities that do not match. If we have no idea of our personal mission statement, it does not make us second-class Christians, but having one can be a catalyst for greater fruitfulness and fulfilment. It is an aspiration worth pursuing.

This is part of our journey of becoming more integrated, enabling us to see an overview of our lives and how our work and vocation are part of life. A personal mission statement is sufficiently general to cover our work and life, but sufficiently specific to enable us to discern and decide whether certain things fit or not. It should be simple, easily understood and compelling, moving us towards working and living with greater purpose. When we are working in the area of our personal mission, work, life, meaning and fulfilment merge.

Course correction

It was just a passing comment that got Jack thinking. Stan had been chatting with him at a barbecue and as they parted, Stan said, 'I don't know what it is about you, Jack, but I always find you easy to talk to.' Jack had mentioned the comment to Liz on the way home and she agreed that it just about summed him up. 'That's why you have so many people trying to get hold of you. You're a great listener and people trust you.'

As Jack reflected about how he was wired to be a listener, he thought about the job he did and began to realize why he might have such a problem with time management and being late. He just loved people talking to him and found it difficult to cut the conversation. Also, administrative stuff was really not his thing and seemed to take him longer than most people.

At work Jack's best moments were when he was listening to others and drawing them out, and his colleagues knew it. Jack could form a trusted relationship faster than most people and the result was that he could understand people's needs better. That was a valuable asset in a business fighting for customer loyalty. Jack began to think about whether his job responsibilities could be shifted towards his areas of strength.

At church, Jack realized that his involvement with the Friday night youth group had been a mistake, because much of what was needed was people to run activities like orienteering or group games. The group was so noisy and boisterous that time to talk was very limited. He was better suited to a different environment, like playing pool with the young people and getting alongside them on a one-to-one basis. A while ago he had been asked to consider working with the pastoral team. Now he realized that it would probably be a good idea to drop the Friday evening and maybe do some pastoral work instead. It was a better fit.

Setting aside time to reflect specifically on the issue of our personal mission is an important way to become more integrated in work and life. 'We have not received the spirit of the world but the Spirit who is from God, that we may understand what God has freely given us' (1 Corinthians 2:12). Sometimes people hear directly from God in a very clear way about their calling. A classic example of this in the

Bible would be Samuel, who was called to be a prophet. Moses and Gideon are other examples of people called to a specific role. For most of us, though, God's calling is likely to be less dramatic.

A starting point in the process is to ask ourselves some questions to tease out what God has already placed within us:

- When did I feel fulfilled and experience positive fruitfulness?
- What experiences (positive or negative) were formative for me?
- Can I see any patterns emerging that indicate strengths and weaknesses?
- What do I typically talk about if left to my own choice? 'Out of the overflow of the heart the mouth speaks' (Matthew 12:34).
- What do I dream about? What do I imagine? What would I love to do?

The problem with this approach is that it limits us to the lens through which we see ourselves. It takes more than our own perceptions to confirm a calling. The Christian approach to developing a personal mission statement is not just speculation. God gives us other people in our lives to help us discern our mission. Ultimately it is the wider body of Christ who confirm our gifting and calling. 'And all Israel from Dan to Beersheba recognised that Samuel was attested as a prophet of the LORD' (1 Samuel 3:20).

Our discovery process involves reflection, analysis, prayer, inspired insight, discussion, testing and ultimately the confirmation of others. It is a process well worth pursuing in order to develop a clearer sense of purpose and ultimately greater fruitfulness and fulfilment in service.

Insight Capture Questions
1. What experiences of mine might be clues towards understanding my mission?
2. What feedback from others do I have about my gifting and calling?

24. MISSION POSSIBLE?

David . . . served God's purpose in his own generation.
(Acts 13:36)

Having committed my life to Christ in my thirties, it
was not until nearly mid-life that I really began to question
what it was God was calling me to do. I read some books
about making a transition from success to significance and
found that idea compelling. Success is usually temporary,
but significance is more permanent. I wanted to make a
difference for God and do things that would have lasting
impact.

I began by writing down a series of commitments that I
wanted to make – a personal values and commitment statement. Some of these values would be generic to all Christians
and some were unique to me. This is what I wrote on a retreat
in 1997.

I am committed to:

- Following the Lord Jesus Christ as Lord of my life and to
  his priorities for my time, skills and money. I will
  endeavour to hear God's voice through the Word and
  prayer and I will act in obedience.
- Loving Helen as her faithful husband. Developing our
  marriage.
- Creating with Helen a home where people experience
  God's love.
- Encouraging believers to live fruitful and fulfilled lives.
- Communicating God's Word graciously and truthfully.

- Living in community, friendship and accountability with others.
- Knowing Christ as my personal life goal and rejecting all positions, possessions or pleasures as goals.

In my opinion, I am failing to a greater or lesser extent on all of these high-sounding statements, but the point is that I wrote something down as a commitment. Writing things down really forces us to think. To be honest, the fact that other people know about these values makes me feel a bit vulnerable, because I know there is a gap between what I am and what I aspire to be.

However, the really helpful thing is that my commitments give me a basis for choosing priorities. I am far less likely to become a 'plate spinner' with a values statement than without one. When opportunities arise, I can use these values to help decide whether I should accept or decline. When I think about what initiatives I could take in work and life, these commitments give me a framework which focuses me on the right kind of activity and helps me keep myself oriented towards God and my other important relationships.

What they do not do is give me a simple and clear single-sentence definition of my purpose. It was not until I read a book by Laurie Beth Jones called *The Path* that I managed to put together a sentence that I believe summarizes what God is doing with my life.

As I worked on this single sentence, I remembered someone saying, 'One of the marks of a vocation is that you do not have to pursue what you can attract.' This is an interesting test. What does God bring our way when we do not seek it out? I notice, and have sometimes been surprised, that people seek me out for advice. Looking back at my life, I realize that God has used me to advise others. As a parent, a management accountant, a preacher, a mentor and speaker, God has used me to advise people. Writing a book like this is part of that. Eventually I came up with this single-phrase personal mission statement: *to inspire people to make the right choices.*

It is not my role to make the right choice for other people, or to direct them into what choice they should make. My role is to help inspire them to make the right choice. (Incidentally, I do not always make the right choice myself – in fact, my failures are sometimes used to inspire other people to make the right choice!) The best way to make a right choice is to look to God, because he is the source of inspiration.

I tested my mission statement on people who knew me and supported me. They all confirmed that it was true about me and resonated with who I am. Then I felt more confident about moving forward in this personal mission. Confirming and refining your statement based on input from others is an important aspect of discovery. Personal values and mission statements are not engraved in tablets of stone for ever. They are living and may be modified or enhanced in the future as we make deeper levels of discovery.

When we have discovered our personal mission state-ment, it helps us to say 'no' to things that do not fit in. This is a very powerful tool to simplify our lives and achieve greater focus. In my case, because I had previously served as a finance director, I was approached to be the treasurer of various organizations (I was already treasurer in my local church). God showed me that this was not to be my main focus. So I declined treasury roles and eventually handed over the local church treasurer role to someone else.

Just let me sound a note of caution, though. Legalism is a great risk for Christians and discovering a personal mission statement carries with it the risk that we become overly narrow about what we choose to do. It is just a tool, not a rule. Everyone has to help 'do the dishes' sometimes and a personal mission statement is not an excuse to bunk off when your service is needed. Jesus' high calling to bring salvation and the kingdom of God did not stop him washing the feet of the disciples. Neither should our mission statements excuse us from giving help where it is needed.

New insights – new roles

Jack looked at his scrappy piece of paper with its crossings out. He had finally arrived at a single sentence: *My personal mission is to enable others to feel accepted and valued by listening to them*. Liz thought it was quite good and others agreed. 'Sounds like you to me,' Mike said.

Jack had no idea how much that sentence would impact his life. When he mentioned it to his boss as part of a discussion on his development plan, it led to him being assigned to handle angry customers, a role in which he excelled. Listening to people who felt they had been ignored was his forte – he had finally found a niche in the organization. After dealing with Jack, disgruntled customers often continued with repeat business.

At church he discussed his profile with the leadership and was glad to join the welcoming team. Liz and Jack were good hosts, and offering hospitality gave him the opportunity to listen to new people and help them feel accepted and valued in the church, something that positively affected church growth. He also found he had a knack for interviewing people in the morning service, putting them at ease and enabling them to share what God was doing in their lives.

Jack was looking at things through a new insight that had given him greater meaning and mission. His focus enabled him to reduce or drop some things that had overloaded his life, creating a better sense of harmony and integration. He felt more fulfilled and more fruitful. Jack's personal mission statement didn't make him perfect, though. He still had a tendency to allow people to talk too much, which meant he was still inclined to be late, and it still took him too long to fix things that broke at home.

It takes time and effort to discover our own personal mission, but once we have discerned it and tested it, we can begin to see all our work, paid and unpaid, through the same lens. We can share our personal mission with others, which helps them understand how to support and encourage us. Developing our personal mission is one of the most powerful ways to bring work and life into alignment, into an integrated whole in the context of God's mission on earth. Finding ourselves and our role within the greatest story ever told is a continuation of Jesus' mission, a wonderful privilege that gives our lives meaning. At the end of his earthly life Jesus said, 'I have brought you glory on earth by completing the work you gave me to do' (John 17:4). Now *that* is something to aim for.

Insight Capture Questions
1. What next step do I want to take to help clarify my personal mission?
2. Who could help me test and affirm my calling and gifting?

25. GROWING UP

I consider my life worth nothing to me, if only I may finish the race and complete the task the Lord Jesus has given me. (Acts 20:24)

Frustration

Cheng hung his head in front of the computer screen and then turned away and wandered over to the window in despair. He had just found out that he had not secured a key position. 'God, how can this be?' he whispered. He placed his hands on the glass and stared at the rain on the window running past his fingers.

He had dreamed of being a doctor since childhood. Something in him recognized it as his calling and he selected his school subjects with medicine in mind. When he just failed to get into medical school the first time, Cheng redoubled his efforts and qualified. Now, aged twenty-seven, after a long training, he had to endure another hold-up. He needed a specialist post to qualify fully and positions were not easy to find. Cheng had been hopeful both of qualifying and of marrying his fiancée next year.

He turned and thumped his hand down onto the desk and slumped into his chair.

Timing can be one of the most difficult things to accept in our growth. God told Samuel to anoint David as king, but years passed before he acceded to the throne (2 Samuel 5:4).

Joseph had a sense of calling when he shared his dreams as a young man (Genesis 37:7), yet his path must have been terribly hard to bear – sold into slavery, falsely accused of rape, imprisoned and then forgotten by the man he helped in jail. Joseph's experiences were extreme examples of frustration and despair. He must have felt that his life was wasting away.

Sometimes it is just a mystery why God allows so many barriers to obstruct our development into the vocation that he has planned for us. Yet during these times of trial God prepares us in a way we are inclined to forget: he prepares our character. He may call us to a role, but our character might not yet be ready. We must mature before we can fully undertake our vocation – the unique work that God has prepared in advance for us to do (Ephesians 2:10).

For both David and Joseph, the school of hard knocks and the university of life helped prepare them for their future roles. David led a group of fighting men and became a respected leader in a difficult environment before being crowned as king. Joseph was given management roles in running both Potiphar's household and a jail, experience that was relevant to his eventual position as Pharaoh's number two. Perhaps only as we look back can we see how God has used delays as a preparation.

Perfect conditions never exist and circumstances are rarely ideal for us to grow in our calling.

> Whoever watches the wind will not plant;
>> whoever looks at the clouds will not reap.
> (Ecclesiastes 11:4)

Growing is not automatic; it is a choice – a choice to respond to what God has revealed and a choice to take the initiative in using our talents to grow in God's purpose for our work and life. Our choice is to make 'the most of every opportunity, because the days are evil' (Ephesians 5:16). Since growth is invariably inhibited or opposed, moving forward means overcoming a whole series of barriers and obstacles. The way we interpret and respond to these blockers is key to our character growth, which is as important as the growth in our mission.

Dreaming

'I don't know how you do it,' said Sarah, shaking her head as she put down the morning coffee. 'Rubbish weather, two kids to look after on your own, a crowded train every day, no bloke to cry on and the boss from hell! You are incredible to stay at this awful place.'

'Thanks!' laughed Becky. 'So what's your escape plan?'

'Well, if you want to know, I'd like to run my own business.'

'Doing what?' asked Becky.

'Selling soft toys,' said Sarah. 'My house is littered with them – I just love making soft toys.'

Becky remembered the gigantic soft Santa that Sarah had brought in at Christmas to auction for charity. She knew Sarah as someone who encouraged and comforted others. In a way, her soft toys were just an extension of that. 'Great,' said Becky. 'Why don't you try it?'

'I don't know. I just don't have the confidence, I suppose.'

'But your husband earns enough to tide you over, doesn't he?'

'Yes, it's not that. I just don't know if I could sell things.'

'Of course you could,' said Becky. 'People were bidding for that soft Santa like crazy. They love that stuff and you make it brilliantly.'

'Yes, but running a business . . . I don't know,' said Sarah. 'I've just never felt I could actually do it, even though I'd love to.'

Moving towards our vocation is an act of faith and faith is needed to overcome self-limiting fears and insecurity in our minds. We may have a sense of what God is calling us to do, but be trapped by a self-image that is a barrier in the mind. That limiting self-image can be age, family background, past failures or comments people have made in the past (such as 'you're no good', or 'you'll never achieve anything'). God seems to specialize in using people who feel weak. 'God chose the weak things of the world to shame the strong' (1 Corinthians 1:27).

Gideon is a classic example of someone limited by his self-image. The story of Gideon's courageous leadership of Israel to overcome the enemy Midianites and Amalekites starts with him hiding in a wine vat. When the angel of the Lord calls him to 'save Israel out of Midian's hand' (Judges 6:14), he replies, 'My clan is the weakest in Manasseh, and I am the least in my family.' That is what he thinks of himself – that he is a nobody who cannot do anything. Gideon's journey of faith is characterized by a gradually increasing conviction that God is with him and will overcome his inadequacy. Eventually Gideon leads just three hundred men and routs thousands with God's direction and help.

Today, a whole self-help industry has grown up around the idea of freeing ourselves from self-limiting beliefs, unleashing our potential and discovering the 'divine within us'. It is all part of what Abraham Maslow called 'self-actualization' and is put at the top of his hierarchy of psychological needs. This is a hugely attractive idea that contains within it the lure of autonomy to determine our own destiny and greatness. It is an echo of the ancient lie of the serpent in the Garden of Eden, who promised Eve that she would 'be like God' (Genesis 3:5).

For the Christian, the summit is not 'self-actualization', but service – service for God and service to others. Growing in our personal mission only makes sense in the context of growing as part of God's mission.

> The Son of Man did not come to be served, but to serve, and to give his life as a ransom for many.
> (Matthew 20:28)

> Each of you should use whatever gift you have received to serve others, faithfully administering God's grace in its various forms.
> (1 Peter 4:10 NIVI)

As John Wesley said, 'Do all the good you can, in all the ways you can, to all the souls you can, in every place you can, at all the times you can, with all the zeal you can, as long as ever you can.'

This idea of serving others has been overtaken by a culture in which people 'self-actualize' as consumers. Those who have made enough money increasingly opt for a 'cruise-control' lifestyle, where leisure interests divert all their attention. We can see this trend over the last twenty years as many volunteer organizations have collapsed. For us to grow in our calling means guarding against a tendency to vegetate.

> Therefore, I urge you, brothers and sisters, in view of God's mercy, to offer your bodies as living sacrifices, holy and pleasing to God – this is your spiritual act of worship. (Romans 12:1 NIVI)

Are we settling for a second-best life, or a life that fulfils the potential God has placed within us?

Insight Capture Questions
1. What belief may be blocking me from growing in my calling?
2. How could I serve others more effectively in the area of my calling?

26. HELD UP?

Wait for the LORD;
  be strong and take heart
  and wait for the LORD.
(Psalm 27:14)

Blocked?

'Anyway,' said Sarah, 'what about you? What would you love to do if you could?'

'I'd love to be a full-time teacher,' said Becky.

'Really?'

'Yes, I would. I've had a growing conviction about it. I love teaching the kids at church and when they did an analysis of my gifts, teaching came out top. It all points the same way.'

'Go for it!' said Sarah, punching the air.

'I can't,' said Becky, rubbing her thumb and forefinger together. 'I don't have enough money to support myself and the kids during the teacher training.'

Some barriers to growing in our vocation are external. Money was limiting Becky's desire to move into her calling of teaching. Another example of an external barrier might be caring for someone else who is dependent. Or we may have all the right instincts to pursue our vocation, but no obvious opportunity to deploy them, like Cheng.

Confronting a blockage we can do nothing about is a very difficult thing to deal with. Any blocked goal causes anger and it is easy to become angry at our circumstances, or at other people we may perceive as blockages. As we saw in the examples of David and Joseph, at times like these it is good to remember that God's primary goal for us is a Christ-like character – and we are the only people who can block that goal. We need to ask God for his grace (2 Corinthians 12:9). Selwyn Hughes quotes a good definition of grace: 'Grace is the strength God gives us which enables us to live or do as Jesus would do were he in our situation.'

A group of supportive people is always helpful. Other Christians who recognize and agree with our calling can empathize with us, encourage us, think things through with us and pray for us. There may even be some practical help they can offer. God's way is to work in cooperation with others. When people recognize a genuine calling of God, you might be surprised how much support they want to give.

One way for us to grow in our calling is to pray the prayer of Jabez:

Jabez cried out to the God of Israel, 'Oh, that you would bless me and enlarge my territory! Let your hand be with me, and keep me from harm so that I will be free from pain.' And God granted his request.
(1 Chronicles 4:10)

This prayer is in four parts. The first request ('bless me') is for God's supernatural favour. The second request ('enlarge my territory') is for greater opportunity and impact. The third ('let your hand be with me') demonstrates dependence on God, and the fourth ('keep me from harm') is a prayer for protection from temptation and evil. This is a prayer for growth in Jabez's personal mission and we can use the same model in praying for our own growth.

Perhaps the biggest risk in the prayer of Jabez is praying it with distorted motives, especially the desire to increase our own greatness and legacy. Once when I was on a retreat, I was walking in the graveyard of an abbey and noticed a gravestone with two identical names on it. It turned out that a father and a son had been buried there, and the father had named the son after himself, including all his middle names. As I read the names, it seemed to me that the father wanted his own identity to be perpetuated, his own legacy to be extended. Then I looked more closely at the detail and saw from the dates on the tombstone that the son had died before the father. How sad and how poignant a lesson it was: we cannot enlarge our own legacy. God determines our legacy.

The model prayer of Jabez springs from the motive of wanting God to help him do what he was called to do. The heart cry of Jabez was not for his own personal greatness, but for the greatness of God through him. He twinned a prayer for God's enlarged impact with a prayer for his enlarged protection. The great encouragement of the prayer of Jabez is that it is followed by the statement, 'And God granted his request.' It is an affirmation that God is at work around us, in us and through us. It raises the expectation of God's work and life in our work and life.

Taking the plunge

After a train delay, Becky had just endured another insensitive verbal bashing from her boss and was at her desk quietly praying with her eyes shut when Sarah came over. 'Becky, why don't you just give him a piece of your mind?'

'No, I'm OK,' Becky replied quietly. 'It wouldn't be the right thing to do.'

Sarah could see peace in Becky and was amazed. 'How do you do it?' she asked. 'How do you keep going, being so positive in this place, when I know you'd rather not be here?'

Becky looked at her. 'Do you really want to know?' Sarah nodded. 'Let's have lunch together and I'll tell you.'

There was something about Becky that Sarah wanted, and by the time that day was out she understood what and who it was. God had used Becky's character and grace in the situation she was in to reach Sarah.

It was a month later to the day when Becky was called into the boss's office to be made redundant. She was stunned, but relieved to find she would get three months' salary tax free in recognition of her six years of service. When Sarah found out Becky was leaving at the end of the month, she felt sad that her friend was going, but realized that God had just provided some of the money Becky needed to make the switch into teaching. She would have to get interim work for the summer, but would then start her training. It turned out to be the trigger for Sarah to make the jump as well, and she sent Becky a special soft toy when she started her course.

We may be in a blocked position for a long time, but God can also change a situation very quickly, just as he did in Joseph's life. If we keep trusting God and praying, hope is something that never completely dies.

A definite pattern emerges in the book of Acts for the disciples as they move out into their mission. God allows opposition as part of the process of growth. Prayer is followed by power to do God's work and power is followed by persecution. Finally, persecution is followed by perseverance and victory. Then the cycle starts again. For example, in Acts 2 we see the church praying, then miraculous signs being done, then the apostles being arrested and brought before the authorities. When they persevere and pray again, the power of God enables them to speak boldly, but then they are arrested and flogged. And so it goes on. Prayer, power, persecution, perseverance. This is a repeating pattern we can expect in our own lives as we seek to grow in our mission.

Ultimately, if what we are doing is of God, the Holy Spirit will overcome spiritual opposition. As Gamaliel said in the case of the disciples in Acts,

> Therefore, in the present case I advise you: Leave these men alone! Let them go! For if their purpose or activity is of human origin, it will fail. But if it is from God, you will not be able to stop these men; you will only find yourselves fighting against God.
> (Acts 5:38–39)

Looking back at the experiences of many men and women in Scripture, time and again we see ordinary people doing great things with God. Faith to move forward in our calling is something that has been proved again and again. As it says in Hebrews 11:32–33,

> I do not have time to tell about Gideon, Barak, Samson, Jephthah, David, Samuel and the prophets, who through faith conquered kingdoms, administered justice, and gained what was promised . . .

Though our choice is essential, there is also something inexorable about the people of God growing into their calling. Just as God has brought the light of Christ into our lives, so he also causes us to grow towards that light.

> The path of the righteous is like the first gleam of dawn,
>   shining ever brighter till the full light of day.
> (Proverbs 4:18)

> The LORD will fulfil his purpose for me.
> (Psalm 138:8)

> May the God of peace, who through the blood of the eternal covenant brought back from the dead our Lord Jesus, that great Shepherd of the sheep, equip you with everything good for doing his will, and may he work in us what is pleasing to him, through Jesus Christ, to whom be glory for ever and ever. Amen.
> (Hebrews 13:20–21)

Insight Capture Questions
1. What circumstances are blocking me from fulfilling the calling God has given me?
2. Do I pray along the lines of the prayer of Jabez and ask others to pray?

27. THE GOOD LIFE

'Love the Lord your God with all your heart and with all your soul and with all your mind.' This is the first and greatest commandment. And the second is like it: 'Love your neighbour as yourself.' All the Law and the Prophets hang on these two commandments.
(Matthew 22:37–40)

If you are anything like me, you will have turned to this chapter first, looking for the golden-nugget conclusion, the fast-fix answer to life, the universe and everything. So here it is, the executive summary of the good life. The answer is . . . Shalom. The Hebrew word *Shalom* is normally translated 'peace', but it means much more than that. Shalom also conveys a sense of wholeness, inner rest and relational harmony. Shalom is the hallmark of an integrated whole-life disciple.

The opposite of Shalom is restlessness: the state of dissatisfaction, unease and sense of being incomplete that pervades our world. While Shalom is wholeness, restlessness is disintegration and chaos. In Scripture restlessness is sometimes symbolized by the sea (Jeremiah 49:23). Perhaps that is why in heaven there will be no more sea (Revelation 21:1), because heaven is total Shalom. The integrated work-life looks, feels and is Shalom. It is what we were made for.

Let's begin with typical symptoms of our work-life malaise: over-tiredness, priority conflicts, irritability, strained relationships, dissatisfaction, and so on. We want a quick fix for these things, but there is no quick fix because of what lies at the root of our problems. If we look into our own hearts, we begin to realize that some of our motives are out of line. When we delve deeper, we find we are being driven by desires like approval, financial security, status, ambition, a relationship, sex, autonomy . . . the list is endless. Behind all of these motives lurks the idol of self. The problem is us and we cannot fix ourselves.

God's solution is to take us out of ourselves to love him. To love someone else is to give them your full attention in every possible way, not just emotionally, but also mentally and physically. The great commandment has a keyword repeated three times. That word is *all*. The key principle is 'all-ness', wholeness, entirety. When our heart, mind and will are oriented towards God, when our spirit, soul and body seek him, valuing him above all else and enjoying him, we are in Shalom. The peace and presence of God is the by-product of giving him our whole attention. Loving God involves all our work and life with no hidden compartments. There is no sacred/secular divide.

Work-life integration is not about trying to balance the pressures and conflicts, or measuring how 'balanced' we are; it is about loving the source from which our life springs. We do not construct a whole-life by pursuing desires, piecing together experiences, or planning. We grow into wholeness by being rooted in the life of God and being a channel of that life to the world. 'I am the vine; you are the branches' (John 15:5).

The evidence around and within us is that, like Martha, we are distracted and 'worried and upset about many things' (Luke 10:41). If our life is divided, it is because we have allowed something other than God to get too important. 'Only one thing is needed. Mary has chosen what is better, and it will not be taken away from her' (Luke 10:42). Focusing on the Lord has a way of putting everything back into its

proper perspective. Some things we thought were important become less important. A stillness and order emerge in
the presence of God.

> My heart is not proud, O LORD,
>   my eyes are not haughty;
> I do not concern myself with great matters
>   or things too wonderful for me.
> But I have stilled and quietened my soul;
>   like a weaned child with its mother,
>   like a weaned child is my soul within me.
> O Israel, put your hope in the LORD
>   both now and for evermore.
> (Psalm 131)

The chapters in this book are all practical expansions of this
one over-arching principle of making God our primary
focus, which is what brings the good life of Shalom.

The good life is in Christ

It is impossible for a man or woman to experience true Shalom
without first receiving Christ. 'No-one can see the kingdom
of God without being born again' (John 3:3 NIVI). In receiving
the Spirit of Christ, 'a righteousness from God is revealed, a
righteousness that is by faith' (Romans 1:17), and we are free
from the guilt of failure and our inability to achieve perfec-
tion. The restless world follows the pattern of Adam, who lost
Shalom when he acted independently of God; but we are no
longer 'in Adam', but 'in Christ', 'For you died, and your life is
now hidden with Christ in God' (Colossians 3:3). Christ is now
central to our identity as children of God.

Having received Christ, we have also received a freedom from being controlled by our old nature. 'It is for

freedom that Christ has set us free' (Galatians 5:1). In Christ we are free from doubts about being accepted that cause us to cave in to the culture. Our approval in him supersedes job titles, pay and performance, promotion and publicity. In Christ we are free from having to wear masks caused by pressure to conform or perform. In Christ we have been given freedom from the driving ambition to be significant that fuels our striving and saps our strength through overwork. In Christ the power of the workplace and the culture to conform us to its pattern are neutralized by the cross. 'The world has been crucified to me, and I to the world' (Galatians 6:14). Christ has disarmed the unseen 'powers and authorities . . . triumphing over them by the cross' (Colossians 2:15).

In Christ we have received a new identity that is foundational to integrating work and life as part of our whole-life worship of God. Now, as believers with our identity in Christ, we work and live to serve him, 'as working for the Lord' (Colossians 3:23). He is our Shalom at work and in life.

Our aim is fruitfulness – reproducing the character of Jesus. As Christ's ambassadors, we meet failure with forgiveness, insult with grace and need with compassion. This is no fuzzy excuse for poor productivity, for we are not just a soft touch. We meet delegated responsibility with diligence, deception with honesty, disorder with discipline. We work hard – 'as for the Lord' – and in Christ our work becomes meaningful as an offering to him. Our productivity and wealth are derived from healthy relationships and disciplined working patterns. Through us Christ spreads the aroma of his character, creating a micro-climate of Shalom around us that can influence the entire culture of the workplace.

Jesus changes our perspective on time. In a world desperate to 'pack everything in' and conquer 'time management', we discover that in Christ time is not always linear in the way we think. Our mortal life is lived in moments, cycles and seasons and, mysteriously, Jesus is present in all of them simultaneously. Christ, who is the Alpha and the Omega, is somehow both inside and outside time. All the days of our lives are written in his book, 'before one of them came to be' (Psalm 139:16). He is the God who is, who was and who is to come (Revelation 1:8). The Gospels never describe Jesus in a hurry. He is always present in the moment. As we relax into his perspective on time, we experience Shalom.

In some vehicles you see floating compasses on the dashboard. Whatever angle or direction the road takes, they swing back to point to the magnetic pole. This is a picture of the whole-life Christian, our inner centre reorienting towards the magnetic personality of God in the bumps and diversions of everyday experience. Whatever our situation in work and life we look to him, the source of our life in Christ.

And we, who with unveiled faces all reflect the Lord's glory, are being transformed into his likeness with ever-increasing glory, which comes from the Lord, who is the Spirit.
(2 Corinthians 3:18)

The good life is in relationships
The good life is lived in relationships, first with God, secondly with a supportive community of believers, and finally in the wider world and workplace. This is how Jesus lived and still lives.

The good life is interspersed with solitudes of communion with the Father, rhythms of connection that sustain us in the desert experience of the world.

O God, you are my God,
earnestly I seek you;

my soul thirsts for you,
  my body longs for you,
in a dry and weary land
  where there is no water.
(Psalm 63:1)

Through the Word and Spirit we experience the mind of Christ (1 Corinthians 2:16) and are comforted, strengthened and encouraged. Time out with God fills us with invisible, refreshing, inspiring Shalom.

The good life is lived in a family of believers, the corporate expression of Christ 'with skin on'. The church family and community provide both the emotional support and empathy we need and the teaching and opportunity to forge the defining values in our lives. It is with close friends in the community that we share our lives, confess our sins and experience accountability. Communities of believers are part of a fallen world, imperfect and riddled with sin, yet Christ amazingly works through them. As we serve and grow, other believers confirm the gifts and calling that serve the body and the wider world. The community of believers reflect the attributes of Christ to us, like many points of light, helping us to navigate through life. In this way we live in relationship with God through the church. In the community of the saints, Shalom is shared.

In our relationships with the world, Christ's experience becomes our experience, our lives contain echoes of his earthly life. Christ lived and lives in a fallen world and workplace. Flawed authority structures, oppressive systems and faulty organizations are the context for our discipleship in the workplace and the world. We sometimes seem to be living a second-choice life with a third-choice job in a spiritual battle.

The interaction of our new and old natures creates conflict in our minds, emotions and choices. 'For the sinful nature desires what is contrary to the Spirit, and the Spirit what is contrary to the sinful nature' (Galatians 5:17). Prompted by the situations we encounter, we are tempted to gain acceptance by conforming to certain working patterns or incentives. Old motivations to satisfy our own needs battle against Christ in us. We want to make a name for ourselves, to amass prosperity and enjoy it, to pretend that money is the answer. Ambition, insecurity and financial pressure all wage war against our souls. Our sinful nature struggles against us with the deception that life can be found by acting independently of God. We fall, we confess and repent, and by God's grace we get up. And somehow in the midst of the battle between our sinful nature and the Spirit is the realization that someone bigger than us is in charge. The victory that is his and has become ours through him brings the Shalom of Christ.

Every time we choose, even in a small way, to alter our choices in line with God's patterns, Shalom advances. As we force ourselves to disengage from an unhealthy work intensity to take just five minutes out with God, Shalom advances. As we make ourselves open, accountable and vulnerable, Shalom advances. As we pause momentarily after someone has said something that really hurt, and with the forgiveness and grace of God say something kind, Shalom advances. When those strong emotions surge within us and we take time out with God to understand why, and take captive those thoughts to Christ, Shalom advances. When by faith we make choices that dethrone the deceptive and subtle control of money, Shalom advances.

Each of the key relationships in our lives tests our worship and our true motivation. Demands from work, home and church clash and we look to finesse the impossible. Jesus refused to be interrupted in his teaching by his mother and brothers waiting outside, yet when he was in the middle of his most intense work on the cross he asked his best friend to look after his mother. That shows me that the right choice is not always the same choice in every circumstance. Some express disappointment about our choices and our hearts shrink with sadness if we are misunderstood. Yet when our choices honour God, Shalom is advancing.

We pray for God to work through us, and in some way he does. Someone is helped, encouraged, empowered – and then almost immediately something negative slaps us down. Something or somebody from outside causes pain and disruption and we echo the unanswered question of Jesus on the cross: 'My God, my God, why have you forsaken me?' (Matthew 27:46) We experience the cycle of prayer, power, persecution and perseverance that is the pattern of discipleship. Like Christ, we learn obedience through what we suffer (Hebrews 5:8), and reluctantly accept that God is disciplining us for our good, even though it does not feel like it (Hebrews 12:10). In the midst of this melee of work and life, Shalom is advancing.

The good life is in grace

The good life is lived in a continual awareness of the grace of God. Grace warms our hearts and astonishes our minds with the realization of God's mercy and forgiveness. We are grateful to the one who has every reason to distance himself from us, but has incredibly chosen the opposite. The greatness of his heart of love overcomes our own sense of inadequacy. 'The grace of our Lord was poured out on me abundantly, along with the faith and love that are in Christ Jesus' (1 Timothy 1:14). Grace makes us worthwhile people.

This good life of grace overflows to others and enables us to accept them as they are. Grace changes how we relate to our demanding boss, our difficult co-workers, the family members we would not choose and the 'awkward squad' in life who pop up now and again in various guises. As we encounter difficulty and ask for more grace, we realize that God is giving us a power far exceeding our own resources and the same grace that saved us is also sustaining us: 'yet not I, but the grace of God that was with me' (1 Corinthians 15:10).

That same dependency on God, which first enabled us to be saved, now enables our work and life. In the quiet obedience of loving and following Jesus and his great commandments, we experience the good life of Shalom.

> Not that I have already obtained all this, or have already been made perfect, but I press on to take hold of that for which Christ Jesus took hold of me. Brothers and sisters, I do not consider myself yet to have taken hold of it. But one thing I do: Forgetting what is behind and straining towards what is ahead, I press on towards the goal to win the prize for which God has called me heavenwards in Christ Jesus.
> (Philippians 3:12–14 NIVI)

Wherever we are in work and life, the grace of God allows us to move on from what is behind and press on towards God. In school races I have noticed that most people cheer from the sidelines, but the parents of young children often stand behind the finishing line to encourage them. They look back down the track into the faces of their children. God our Father is looking into our faces with his arms outstretched as we move towards him through life, sometimes running, sometimes stumbling, but advancing in his grace and Shalom.

We are like Peter gazing at Christ, walking towards him on the restless sea. We are navigating this life amidst the tension of conflicting expectations, on the restless sea of circumstances, focused on Jesus. We do not seek Shalom; we seek our God who brings us Shalom. When Peter famously takes his eyes off Jesus for a moment, he sinks, but the great thing is that the story does not end there. Jesus, who has dominion over the forces of chaos, reaches out and pulls him back up. Such is the grace of our God.

> The LORD sits enthroned over the flood;
>> the LORD is enthroned as King for ever.
> The LORD gives strength to his people;
>> the LORD blesses his people with Shalom.
> (Psalm 29:10–11)

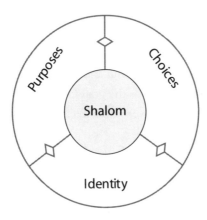

Figure 9. Work/Life harmony

NOTES

To avoid intrusion, the author's sources have not been cited in the text. The following notes, however, identify his sources, and may be useful for further exploration of the chapter themes.

Chapter 3: Wisdom for the way
Elliott, Clifford. *With Integrity of Heart. Living Values in Changing Times*. Friendship Press, 1991.
Warren, Rick. *The Purpose Driven Life*. Zondervan, 2002.

Part 1: Living Authentically
Rowell, Gill. *The Spiritual @dventures of CyberCindy*. Paternoster Press, 2003.

Chapter 4: Who do you think you are?
Kremen Bolton, Nancy. *The Third Shift*. Jossey Bass, 2000.
Anderson, Neil T. *Victory over the Darkness*. Regal Books, 1992. Reprinted 2000.

Chapter 5: Afraid or authentic?
Nee, Watchman. *The Normal Christian Life*. Kingsway, 1963.
Thomas, Viv. *Second Choice*. Paternoster, 2000.
Anderson, Neil T. *The Freedom in Christ Discipleship Course*. Monarch, 2004.
Shattock, Geoff. *Worktalk*. New Wine, 2003. www.worknetuk.org

Chapter 6: Connected in community
Vanier, Jean. *Community and Growth*. Dartman, Longman & Todd, 1979.

MacDonald, Gordon. *A Resilient Life*. STL, 2004.

Featherby, James. *Join a Band: Being Church in the City*. X1, 2005.

Chapter 10: The naked truth?

Rogers, Henry J. *The Silent War*. New Leaf Press, 1999.

Arterburn, Stephen and Stoeker, Fred. *Every Man's Battle*. Waterbrook Press, 2000.

Roberts, Ted. *Pure Desire*. Regal Books, 1999.

Chapter 11: Who can I trust?

www.licc.org.uk

Chapter 12: Breaking the power of money

Foster, Richard. *Money, Sex and Power*. Hodder and Stoughton, 1985.

Foster, Richard. *Freedom of Simplicity*. Hodder and Stoughton, reprinted 2005.

Chapter 13: Beyond my means?

Consumer credit advice in UK: 0800 1381111

www.creditaction.org.uk

Parsons, Rob. *The Money Secret*. Hodder and Stoughton, 2005.

Chapter 15: Got rhythm?

Marmot, Michael. *Status Syndrome – How Your Social Standing Directly Affects Your Health*. Bloomsbury, 2005.

Tricordant Ltd. *Healthy Work for Whole People*. 2006.

Schumacher, Christian. *God in Work*. Lion, 1998.

Chester, Tim. *The Busy Christian's Guide to Busyness*. IVP, 2006.

The Relationships Foundation. www.relationshipsfoundation.org

Chapter 16: High time

Swindoll, Chuck. *Intimacy with the Almighty*. STL, 1996.

Chapter 19: Finding a fit
Veal, Debra. *Rowing it Alone*. Robson Books, 2002.

Chapter 20: What do you really want?
Hillman, Os. *Making Godly Decisions: How to Know and Do the Will of God*. Aslan Group, 2004.

Lord, Peter. *Hearing God*. Baker Book House, 1998.

Chapter 21: Common sense?
Lucado, Max. *The Great House of God*. W Publishing Group, 2001.

Hillman, Os. *Making Godly Decisions: How to Know and Do the Will of God*. Aslan Group, 2004.

Parsons, Rob. *The Heart of Success*. Hodder and Stoughton, 2002.

Willard, Dallas. *Hearing God*. IVP, 1984.

Chapter 22: Spirited conviction
Wallis, Arthur. *God's Chosen Fast*. Kingsway, 1969.

Foster, Richard. *Celebration of Discipline*. Hodder and Stoughton, 1989.

Chapter 23: Why am I here?
The idea of 'a called person' originates from MacDonald, Gordon. *Ordering Your Private World*. Highland, 1985.

Guiness, Os. *The Call*. Word Publishing, 1998.

Chapter 24: Mission possible?
MacDonald, Gordon. ibid.

Dewar, Francis. *Called or Collared?* SPCK, 1991.

Parsons, Rob. *The Heart of Success*. Hodder and Stoughton, 2002.

Warren, Rick. *The Purpose Driven Life*. Zondervan, 2002.

Jones, Laurie Beth. *The Path*. Hyperion, 1996.

Buford, Bob. *Half Time*. HarperCollins, 1997.

Sine, Tom and Christine. *Living on Purpose*. Monarch, 2002.

Bird, Matt. *Destiny*. Hodder and Stoughton, 2000.

Chapter 25: Growing up

Peterson, Eugene. *Leap Over a Wall*. Harper San Francisco, 1997.

Chapter 26: Held up?

Buford, Bob. *Stuck in Half Time*. Zondervan, 2001.

Wilkinson, Bruce. *The Prayer of Jabez*. Multnomah, 2000.